J. A. (John Augustus) Spalding

From New England to the Pacific

Notes of a Vacation Trip across the Continent in April, May, and June, 1884

J. A. (John Augustus) Spalding

From New England to the Pacific
Notes of a Vacation Trip across the Continent in April, May, and June, 1884

ISBN/EAN: 9783337148218

Printed in Europe, USA, Canada, Australia, Japan

Cover: Foto ©Andreas Hilbeck / pixelio.de

More available books at **www.hansebooks.com**

From New England to the Pacific.

Notes of a Vacation Trip Across the Continent in April, May, and June, 1884.

J. A. S., in Hartford Evening Post.

HARTFORD, CONN.:
PRESS OF THE CASE, LOCKWOOD & BRAINARD CO.
1884.

REMARK.

The thirteen letters which constitute this volume were originally contributed to THE HARTFORD EVENING POST by one of the representatives of that journal whose good fortune it was to be also a member of the Raymond Excursion Party which left Boston for the Pacific Coast on the 24th of April last. The letters were not written with reference to any further publication, and they appear in this form solely through respect of the writer for the wishes of those of the party who could not be supplied with files of THE POST containing the full series.

J. A. S.

HARTFORD, June 30, 1884.

PERSONNEL.

W. RAYMOND,	Boston, Mass., Manager.
C. C. HARDING,	Boston, Mass., In Charge.
H. A. TITUS,	Bellows Falls, Vt., Assistant.
H. H. FULLAM,	Concord, N. H., Assistant.
Almy, Chas. T.,	Tilton, N. H.
Andrews, S. C.,	Worcester, Mass.
Andrews, Mrs. S. C.,	Worcester, Mass.
Andrews, Thomas E.,	Holliston, Mass.
Andrews, Mrs. Thomas E.,	Holliston, Mass.
Bacon, Mrs. J. E.,	Worcester, Mass.
Bradley, H. O.,	Worcester, Mass.
Bradley, Mrs. H. O.,	Worcester, Mass.
Brown, Mrs. Mary S.,	Lynn, Mass.
Ball, Sidney A.,	Carlisle, Mass.
Chase, Mrs. S. A. D.,	Roxbury, Mass.
Cox, Rev. Samuel,	Newtown, N. Y.
Cox, Mrs. Samuel,	Newtown, N. Y.
Craven, John V.,	Salem, N. J.
Denison, Miss T. A.,	Springfield, Mass.
Fish, Daniel W.,	Brooklyn, N. Y.
Goodspeed, Dr. Helen A.,	Worcester, Mass.
Grout, Mrs. Mary J.,	Worcester, Mass.
Hamilton, S.,	Pittsburgh, Pa.
Hamilton, Mrs. S.,	Pittsburgh, Pa.
Hamilton, Master,	Pittsburgh, Pa.
Hamilton, Master,	Pittsburgh, Pa.

Howe, George,	Lynn, Mass.
Howe, Mrs. George,	Lynn, Mass.
Kimball, Miss J. W.,	Worcester, Mass.
Knowlton, A.,	West Gardner, Mass.
Longman, Mrs. Kate,	Brooklyn, N. Y.
Marx, Hon. Guido,	Toledo, Ohio.
Marx, Mrs. Guido,	Toledo, Ohio.
Marx, Miss Ella,	Toledo, Ohio.
Massey, Mrs. L. D.,	Danvers, Mass.
Merriman, E. A.,	Meriden, Conn.
Merriman, Mrs. E. A.,	Meriden, Conn.
Mills, Hiram F.,	Lawrence, Mass.
Mills, Mrs. Hiram F.,	Lawrence, Mass.
McCulloch, Mrs. L. S.,	Stevens Point, Wis.
Nichols, Chas. H.,	Boston, Mass.
Nichols, Mrs. Chas. H.,	Boston, Mass.
Pinney, C. H., M.D.,	Derby, Conn.
Pinney, Mrs. C. H.,	Derby, Conn.
Reed, Miss Sophia,	Lynn, Mass.
Richards, F. C.,	Boston, Mass.
Riedler, Max,	Boston, Mass.
Shattuck, H. B.,	Lowell, Mass.
Shattuck, Miss Bertha C.,	Lowell, Mass.
Spalding, J. A.,	Hartford, Conn.
Taft, Mrs. Calvin,	Worcester, Mass.
Talbot, Seth, Jr.,	Tremont, Ill.
Talbot, Mrs. Seth, Jr.,	Tremont, Ill.
Tenney, Alfred E.,	Providence, R. I.
Valpey, H. R.,	Lynn, Mass.
Valpey, Mrs. H. R.,	Lynn, Mass.
Whidden, Thomas J.,	Boston, Mass.
Whidden, S. H.,	Boston, Mass.
Williams, Mrs. J. M.,	Worcester, Mass.
Worcester, Rev. J. H.,	Burlington, Vt.
Worcester, Mrs. J. H.,	Burlington, Vt.

CONTENTS.

I.	First Notes of the Journey,	9
II.	From Chicago to Colorado,	18
III.	In and About Denver,	31
IV.	Up Among and Over the Rockies,	45
V.	Deserts, Flowers, Orange Groves, Vineyards,	67
VI.	Delightful Days at Los Angeles,	80
VII.	Tehachapi Pass and the Sierra Nevadas,	94
VIII.	The California of '49 and '84,	108
IX.	The Sundries of San Francisco,	126
X.	Menlo Park and Santa Clara Valley,	139
XI.	A Long-to-be-Remembered Week,	153
XII.	Good-Bye to San Francisco,	166
XIII.	The Backward Journey—Home Again,	185

I.

FIRST NOTES OF THE JOURNEY—*The Start— The Party—In a Pullman Sleeper—The Route—Chicago and its Characteristics—Becoming Well Acquainted.*

> SHERMAN HOUSE, CHICAGO, ILL.,
> April 27, 1884.

And this is Chicago; great, bustling, grimy, wicked Chicago. I came in yesterday at its back door, as one must enter every city who enters it by railroad; and the back door of Chicago is not unlike that of a hundred other American cities, with its uncanny brats, its squalid women, its miserable hovels, and its irrepressible goat. In approaching Boston, for miles in any direction the observer is favored with a distinct view of the city in wonderful and charming detail; in approaching Chicago, only an impenetrable cloud of smoke indicates its locality, completely enveloping and obscuring from remote view every object, however otherwise prominent. This omnipresent smoke is a feature of Chicago existence. It comes from the universal combustion of their bituminous coal. It impregnates the atmosphere and fills the nostrils with every breath. It begrimes architecture, it invades the inner sanctuary of home to the discomfiture of tidy housekeepers, it precludes the possibility of clean linen, or clean hands, or clean anything, and, to an Eastern man, proves a source of constant discomfort. Doubtless the citizen becomes so accustomed to it as not to be annoyed, although I do not see how he can help regretting that some of the beautiful and costly marble buildings are so stained and aged after a brief exposure to this coal smoke, as to be indistinguishable from commonest stone.

As you will observe from my date, this is

Sunday. I suppose the proper thing for me to do this morning would have been to join the company of worshipers at Dr. Kittridge's. But instead I strolled down Michigan avenue, by the lakeside, past the great exposition building where the national Republican and Democratic Conventions are soon to assemble, through Broadway, over the Randolph street bridge, and after a circuit of eight or ten miles thus made on foot, feel almost sorry that I did not adopt the more restful plan of my friend Mr. Fish, who spent his hour on the cushions of the sanctuary above alluded to. In my profane tramp I have noticed that a Christian observance of the Sabbath is not the fashion in Chicago. There seems to be no general suspension of business. Of course the street and railroad cars run as often as on any other day, but stores, and offices, and shops are open and doing business, loaded trucks and express wagons are busy, hucksters cry their wares on the sidewalks, and there is very little to distinguish Sunday from the day last preceding.

I spent two or three hours yesterday among public buildings and getting impressions of men and things in this incomprehensible city. I saw the three-million-dollar county building on Randolph street, with its eighty odd rooms, in all but a half a dozen of which they have to keep gas burning because insufficient daylight enters through the oddly placed windows. I passed over the long bridge which crosses the railroads converging here, and counted sixty-three sets of tracks running side by side beneath it. I went through some of the elegant apartments of the Grand Pacific Hotel, and for a moment interviewed one of the royally arrayed clerks, who evidently wouldn't swap places with the Czar of all the Russias. I looked down (as far as the smoke would permit) the magnificent distance of Michigan avenue—seven miles as straight as an arrow, and flat as a floor. I crossed the beautifully located but sadly neglected park just below the Baltimore & Ohio Railroad station, to one of the wharves, and enjoyed a half hour on board a little excursion steamer, taking in a trip around "The Pier" at an expense of a dime. I looked in vain for a transparent drop of the clay-colored waters of Lake Michigan as they rippled beneath the guards of the little steamer or rested untouched in my goblet at the dinner table. I paused occasionally on the street to attempt a mental analysis of the economy of wooden pavements and sidewalks of the same material. But I pondered longest over the fearful and wonderful make-up of the Chicagoan, himself and herself. He, lacking the infinite repose of the solid and methodical Bostonian, as well as the resolute promptness and tireless activity of the representative New York business man, is something so thoroughly American that, whether rampant or couchant, he has the appearance of being in his accomplishments a constant surprise to himself, as he certainly is to the slower going world outside. And she—what shall I say of her? In dress she adopts the fancies of every nation under the sun, with a preponderance of neither; in form and manner she is natural to the last degree; in mind and feature prepossessing, though in unaccountable contrast with her local contemporaries of the other sex; and as to the peculiarity of her gait, it is proverbial that nature has been generous to the Chicago woman, which is all that need be said on that subject.

But I am spending too much time in Chicago, without saying a word of how or why I happen to be here. It is my good fortune to be one of sixty-three New Englanders who, some weeks ago, decided on a junketing trip to Colorado and California, under the special charge of Mr. W. Raymond of Boston, whose name and fame in such connection are household words throughout the

East. In accordance with his plan, Greenfield, Mass., was made the place of rendezvous, and on the evening of Thursday, April twenty-fourth, the sixty odd gentlemen and ladies made successful departure from that place in three Pullman palace sleepers, attached to the regular Pacific Express over the New York, West Shore & Buffalo Railroad. Among the members of the party whose names you will recognize, are Mr. and Mrs. S. C. Andrews, Mr. and Mrs. H. O. Bradley of Worcester, Mr. and Mrs. E. A. Merriman of Meriden, Mr. and Mrs. H. F. Mills of Lawrence, Dr. and Mrs. C. H. Pinney of Derby, Mr. H. B. Shattuck and daughter of Lowell, Mr. A. E. Tenney of Providence, Mr. T. J. Whidden and son of Boston, and your correspondent of Hartford. Mr. Max Reidler of Boston, one of Messrs. Prang & Co's well-known artists, is also among the party, and has afforded us no small degree of pleasure by his happy portraits and caricatures of the excursionists in their respective attitudes and habiliments. To many the first night's experience in a sleeping car was a novelty, and the preparations for retiring were, perhaps, less complete than they would have been under other circumstances. In general, however, the situation was accepted philosophically, and subsequent events have shown how easily one may accustom himself or herself to what has seemed unpleasant in anticipation, after once the inauguration is over. Our full train consisted of fourteen Pullman cars, and the route, as far as Buffalo, was near to and parallel with the New York Central & Erie Canal. Meals were provided, generally, on itinerary time, at hotels, restaurants, or in the company's dining-cars, and thus far the trip has been very comfortably made, and without any unexpected or unpleasant occurrence. The time has been principally occupied by the excursionists in becoming well acquainted with one another, in which pleasant exercise we have the valnable and gracefully rendered aid of our chief, Mr. Raymond. We reached this city Saturday noon, and are very acceptably quartered at the Sherman House. Eleven o'clock to-morrow morning is the hour assigned for resuming our journey, of which I hope to give you further account in due time.

II.

From Chicago to Colorado—*Historical Ground—The Plains and Dugouts—Pueblo—The Rockies—Pike's Peak—Manitou and its Wonderful Surroundings.*

Manitou, Col., May 1st.

The Raymond Excursion Party reached this point last evening, having made two thousand two hundred and twenty miles of its westward journey from Boston. To proceed chronologically with these notes of our trip, I should say that we left Chicago on Monday morning, over the Chicago, Rock Island & Pacific Railway, making our first stop at Joliet. Here are the extensive quarries which furnish Chicago with its building stone and flaggings. The State penal institutions are also located here. La Salle, with its coal mines, tile factories, and great zinc works, attracted attention, but there was little else of note until, at Moline, our train suddenly rolled up alongside the Mississippi, and five minutes later we were crossing the immense double bridge which connects Illinois with Iowa. This was my first view of the father of American rivers. The stream here is divided by Rock Island, upon which are situated the United States arsenal and machine shops, which were designed to constitute the central and principal government depot of supplies and munitions of war. The wider and navigable portion of the stream is on the west of the island, and from shore to shore the distance is a trifle over a mile. More than an hour was given us in Davenport, which time was occupied by most of the party in a cursory examination of this steady-going city, noted chiefly for being the place where was completed the compact with the Indians which opened up Illinois, Iowa, and Wisconsin to white settlement. During the night we had opportunity to observe a prairie fire some miles southward. Tuesday morning found us at Kansas City, which lies at the junction of the Missouri and Kansas or "Kaw" Rivers. The "Big Muddy" was something of a surprise in its evident inferiority to the Mississippi.

We dined at Topeka, having passed through Lawrence, leaving Leavenworth and Atchison at the north of us. This is historical ground, and the familiar names of localities in this part of Kansas brought vividly to mind the times and events of Missouri border ruffians, and of "old John Brown," before the inauguration of the war of the Rebellion. At Carbondale our heavy train was "stalled" for a few minutes on a steep grade, giving us opportunity to observe the numerous coal mines. Strata of bituminous coal underlie all this part of Kansas at a depth of from two to twenty feet. The natives state that in some places the farmers come upon the upper stratum in plowing for their crops. For the next three hundred miles the road lies through a region of rich, black bottom lands, in which are wheat fields and corn fields covering thousands upon thousands of acres, all flat and wet and black, scarcely any other animal to be seen than the universal and inevitable black hog, dirty and repulsive to the last degree. Occasional orchards show that fruit may be made to grow, but as a rule these lands are treeless. The farm-houses are generally one-story huts; there are next to no roads, and very few fences. Western Kansas, in striking contrast with that portion just passed over, is dry and well-nigh barren. Thorough desolation seems to mark our route for thirty hours, or almost up to Pueblo in Colorado, full five hundred miles. On both sides the view to the horizon is unbroken by tree, or shrub, or hillock, and the sandy surface shows only occasional patches of the short buffalo-grass to furnish anything like grazing for the cattle which roam over it. Sage brush of a few inches growth, prickly pear scarce showing above the sand, and the bayonet grass in little green shoots, are the only evidences of vegetable life observable. The great want is water. Where irrigation is introduced, there springs an oasis. Occasionally a sluggish stream meanders across the plains, and its course is always marked by the millions of cattle grazing upon its banks, dotting the plain in line of the watercourse as far as the eye can see. Underlying these plains, at a depth of but a few feet, is a table of limestone, and immediately beneath that is "water, water everywhere." By boring the earth to a depth of eight or ten feet, anywhere within twenty miles of the Arkansas River, abundant water is found, but there is no pressure to bring it to the surface.

Aubrey, where the train stops for water, is a little village of "dugouts," or holes in the earth strongly resembling a receiving-tomb in a New England country cemetery. Probably twenty of these burrows serve to constitute the places of abode of the one hundred inhabitants of Aubrey. I sought to enter one of these dugouts, approaching the door, the upper half of which was glazed, and curtained with a dirty red cotton pocket handkerchief. There was neither latch nor handle, knob nor knocker visible, and the place seemed to be deserted. Pressing against the door, it failed to yield, but the slight noise occasioned a commotion within, and with a sudden movement the red handkerchief was jerked aside, revealing against the glass the gaunt visage of a woman. She gazed for an instant, then dropped the curtain and retreated with such precipitancy, shouting "Murder!" at the top of her voice, that I was only too glad to be with equal precipitancy summoned back to the train by the ringing of the locomotive bell, without continuing my investigations.

We overtook occasional emigrant wagons, in clusters of three or four, all going westward. They look just as they have been a thousand times pictured. Flocks of sheep, without a shepherd, including apparently uncounted thousands, nibble unconcernedly wherever there is herbage to attract them. Who can shear them, in this vast plain where there is not one inhabitant to a square mile! Thousands of timid little prairie dogs pop up their heads, and as suddenly subside within their burrows as the train rushes through the midst of their quiet colonies. I find that this land belongs to Uncle Sam. It is quoted at one dollar and twenty-five cents per acre. It seems strange that anybody should want it at any price.

We breakfast, Wednesday, at Coolidge, the westernmost station in Kansas, and the location of the railroad company's repair shops. It is a little gem of a place, as villages go in this part of the country. West of Coolidge extend the alkaline plains,

white as snow, in the midst of which is Fort
Lyon, where Kit Carson was buried. His
monument is in sight of us, by the river,
surrounded by cottonwoods. Beside the
government buildings here are no other
habitations than half a dozen adobe or mud
huts and a few barracks, dropped down by
the railroad station, amid the desolations of
a Colorado desert.

Fifty miles farther on we come in sight of
the Spanish Peaks of the Rocky Mountains,
with their snowy sides and summits. They
look to be twelve or fifteen miles away, and
members of the party fall to disputing about
the distance between them and us. We consult authority and find it to be seventy miles
as the crow flies. Shortly we reach Pueblo,
the third city in Colorado in point of size
and importance. To our great gratification
a halt of two hours is ordered here, and
after a substantial dinner we are taken in
charge by the Pueblo Board of Trade, who
treat us to a side excursion to the great

smelting works of the Colorado Coal and Iron Company, give us all a carriage drive about their thrifty and attractive city, and otherwise entertain and lionize us in the most approved style. Your correspondent is under special obligation to his honor Mayor Shireman and to President Adams of the Board of Trade, for personal attentions received from each. I could give you a variety of interesting statistics concerning the Coal and Iron Company, and the City of Pueblo, but must content myself with saying that this young western city is head and shoulders above many an eastern town that I know of, in all that goes to constitute commercial greatness or to make one hopeful for its future.

Resuming our places in the cars, the party were soon on the way to Manitou, fifty miles distant, arriving at the Manitou House just after eight in the evening. The village is composed chiefly of hotels and a few private residences, with stores, churches, shops, and a fine bathing establishment. Its permanent population numbers but a few hundreds, yet its hotels are said to entertain fifty thousand visitors yearly. A company of Boston capitalists have purchased a large tract of land here, and are erecting or have completed about fifty elegant cottages at various advantageous points, with bathing-houses, drinking-houses at the springs, and sundry other accessions which will have a certain tendency to make this resort ultimately the Saratoga of the west.

The springs are about a dozen in number. They are principally soda and iron, and their medicinal qualities are such as to give them wide repute. Manitou is six thousand three hundred and fifty-seven feet above the sea. The village is immediately surrounded by mountains, a dozen prominent peaks being in view from my window as I write—the highest being Pike's Peak, fourteen thousand three hundred and thirty-six feet above the sea. These mountains are nearly all covered with snow, and the view is one of unsurpassed grandeur and sublimity. Pike's Peak looms up amid the clouds like a monument of alabaster, reflecting the sun's rays and producing an impression of sublime beauty upon the beholder which is absolutely impossible of adequate description.

Nearly every member of our party joined this morning in an excursion by carriages to some of the chief places of interest in this immediate vicinity, including the Garden of the Gods, Glen Eyrie, Mushroom Park, the Rainbow Falls, the Ute Iron Springs, Williams Cañon, and the Cave of the Winds. The Garden of the Gods is considered the most wonderful of all, although I found the surroundings of Rainbow Falls and Williams Cañon scarcely less wonderful or impressive. The mountains and cañons and gorges of Manitou I can only think of in comparison or contrast with our own White Mountain scenery, which latter is, I must confess, so far eclipsed by what I have seen here, as to leave of them for me only a sad memory. The other wonders of sandstone turrets and domes and fantastic rock-forms rising abruptly four or five hundred feet, and scattered like sentinels about the plains at the feet of these mountains, and within these broad cañons, are comparable to nothing I have heretofore seen, and they exceed in their grotesqueness and sublimity the ideal which my imagination had constructed. We start to-morrow morning for a two days' trip to Denver, and among the gold mines of Gilpin County; but I am in love with Manitou, and happy in the thought that two whole days of next week will be allowed us for a further exploration of the wonderful and beautiful objects and localities with which this region abounds. I have just spoken of the White Mountains. My recollection is that the summit of Mount Washington is scarce six thousand feet high. The lowest spot in this village is over six thousand feet, and Pike's Peak towers in front of us eight thousand two hundred and twelve feet higher still! There is a government signal station at the summit of Pike's Peak. Yesterday a signal of distress was displayed at the station, and two parties have set out to attempt to reach and relieve the occupant. The snow between "timber line" and the summit is from thirty to fifty feet deep, yet with the aid of their snowshoes and other appliances the rescuers expect to be able to reach the station within twenty-four hours of the start. I shall probably write you next from Santa Fé.

III.

IN AND ABOUT DENVER—*Silver Mining and Smelting—Up Clear Creek Gulch—Central City and its Mines—Elevated Railroading—Colorado Springs.*

COLORADO SPRINGS, COL., May 4.

Friday and Saturday, May second and third, were assigned for a visit to Denver and the mining regions northwest up Clear Creek fifty miles into the heart of the Rockies of Jefferson and Gilpin Counties. On the morning of Friday we left Manitou, bright and early, and before noon had covered the eighty-odd miles intervening between our starting point and the Queen City. We approached Denver by the way of Jewel Park, bisecting the familiar "Circle Road" in which your late Governor

Jewell was once financially interested. The city is spread out over the plains at the foot of the everlasting hills, both Pike's Peak, at the south, and Long's Peak, at the north, being within easy view. The people of Denver have a right to be, as they are, very proud of their city. It is said to contain sixty thousand inhabitants. Its streets are broad, and, though not paved, do not appear to be subject to the annoyance of mud or excessive roughness. Broadway extends thirteen miles, from north to south, within the city limits, straight and level. It is illuminated by night by electric lights from several towers in different portions of the city, these towers being two hundred feet high, and each having a cluster of twelve burners. Even in the business portions of the city, and particularly on those streets where the homes of the people are situated, there is an air and appearance of cleanliness and sweetness, as well as of elegance and luxury, which is in striking contrast with most cities of its magnitude, East or West. Outside the very heart of the city, the streets are all lined with cottonwoods and maples, and the lawns and gardens abound with fruit trees, whose growth is made possible only by the system of irrigation which brings the waters of the Platte into the city by canals and distributes them through every street. Little rivulets thus fill the gutters, cooling the atmosphere, penetrating the thirsty earth, and giving vigor to every variety of vegetation within reach of its moisture. Numerous artesian wells supply pure and healthful water for domestic purposes.

The architecture of Denver is its most impressive characteristic. This feature shows itself as the visitor alights from the railroad train and finds confronting him the stately "Union Depot," built of pink and white sandstone, a marvel of elegance and completeness, one of the very largest and finest railroad stations in America. Other conspicuous edifices are the Tabor Opera House, said to be the finest opera house in the country, the Windsor and St. James Hotels (at the latter of which the Raymond Excursion Party were quartered), the Court House and City Hall, Tabor Block, La Veta Palace, the Exposition Building, Colorado National Bank Block, St. John's Cathedral, etc. On Capitol Hill are a large number of elegant private residences. There are said to be over a hundred of these which cost more than eighty thousand dollars each. The prevailing building material is brick, although the most expensive structures are of the beautiful pink and salmon tinted sandstone, a material which produces the very choicest effects in the hands of a tasty and skillful architect. Here are no less than fifty-four churches and thirty-three institutions of learning, which fairly indicates the character and intellectual inclinations of the people. The city and its suburbs are brought into proximity by numerous lines of street cars and narrow-gauge railroads; the telephone is here; so is the district messenger service. There are four daily newspapers, and each appears to be well conducted and liberally sustained. Indeed, the city has all modern improvements and advantages possessed by any other city on the continent. Almost the sole business of its inhabitants is mining. Strangers have come here from every portion of the country, have found fortunes in the mountains or adjoining plains, have spent their money here, and the result is—simply Denver; and there is no other Denver in the world.

The Connecticut members of the party spent an hour at the extensive works of the Boston and Colorado Smelting Company, owned by Boston capital and officered, mainly, by New England men. We had the satisfaction of observing every operation required in reducing rough quartz to refined gold and silver, and of bringing away some handsome specimens of the finished product of the establishment. Among the interesting objects seen in the refining-room were twenty-one pure silver bricks, just "poured," worth two thousand three hundred dollars each; and a great tank in which reposed one hundred and fifty thousand dollars worth of "sponge silver" awaiting the roaster. The annual product of these smelting works is about four million dollars of silver, two million dollars of gold, and one million dollars of copper.

Having seen, in Denver, something of what wealth in gold and silver may accomplish, we were ready, Saturday morning, for a trip among some of the hiding-places of the precious metals in their crude and original form. Our destination was Black Hawk and Central City, forty miles up the "Wonder Railroad," as this narrow gauge branch of the Colorado Central Railway is very appropriately styled. Sixteen miles away we reach Golden, which lies at the base of the Rocky Mountain foot-hills.

At Golden we enter Clear Creek Gulch, and begin the twenty-six mile climb which will terminate at Central City, three thousand feet nearer heaven. Clear Creek, as it emerges from the gulch or gorge which bears its name, is a rushing, roaring stream, of about the volume of your Park River before the spring freshet has fairly subsided. It may have been "clear" when first named, but the constant disturbance of the soil by miners along its bed, and the discharges of tons and tons of crushed sandstone and limestone quartz into it daily, have brought the stream to about the consistency and color of a regulation dose of calomel and jalap. In the shallow portions of this stream, all the way up to Black Hawk, may be seen hundreds of Chinamen, wearing high rubber boots, washing for gold. Some of them erect long, narrow flumes, or sluices, through which little streams of water are made to run less rapidly than in the river-bed. Minute particles of gold and silver in the water are thus deposited on the bottom of the sluice, and once a week, or oftener, the little stream is shut off, and the bottom of the sluice is washed for the precious metals. The natives tell us that the soil up and down the bed of this creek has been handled over and over again within the last thirty years, but it still yields something. Even after so many washings, the Chinamen find from two to five dollars a day. The race are natural scavengers, and better satisfied to wade the streams for "tailings" than to labor for wages in the mines above. Occasionally we pass men working with pick or spade in the mountain side, digging little holes here and there, wherever earth shows itself among the rocks. These are surface miners, and their tedious labor is occasionally rewarded by a "find." We were shown a pint or more of gold nuggets at one of the banks in Central City, varying in size from a buckshot to an old-fashioned copper cent, which had been found by surface miners along this gulch. The banks buy the nuggets and the free gold. The nuggets found in Clear Creek Gulch, as I presume elsewhere, are of all conceivable shapes. I saw none larger than thirty-two pennyweights, and most of them were less than one-eighth that size.

The trip up the gulch was something to be remembered. The railway follows the stream, of course, at heights varying from ten to fifty feet above its bed. On either hand the rocky mountain-sides rise more or less abruptly to a height of eight to twelve hundred feet, and the curves are such as would render progress impossible on any other than a narrow gauge. In places the huge rocks actually overhang us a thousand feet above; in others we leap a chasm with only a slight trestle between us and eternity. The trip is made in observation cars. Considering the sharp curves, and the heavy grades, and the constantly threatening features of the road bed, the speed at which the train runs is absolutely terrific. For the first five miles I was in momentary expectation that my life insurance policies were about to become claims; but somehow I managed to get accustomed to the apparent danger, and when, between Black Hawk and Central, the road ascends the last elevation in zizzag, I looked with serenity over the side of the open car to the bottom of the gulch six hundred feet below. These twenty-four miles, grooved in the sturdy foot-hills, illustrate well American railway enterprise. Fourteen trains are run daily over the single track, and notwithstanding the seeming recklessness of management, there has never been a serious accident during the history of the road. The present terminus of this branch is at Central City. Here our party dined at the Teller House, erected by and named in honor of Secretary of Interior Teller, who is a citizen of this place. His unostentatious residence is pointed out to the visitor. The villages of Black Hawk and Central City extend about a mile up the gulch, there being but a single street running longitudinally, and a few short and unimportant ones crossing. The twelve or fifteen hundred inhabitants are miners, representing the sole industry of "the camp," as the natives designate the neighborhood. Central City proper has the post-office, the stores, the three banks, the newspaper, and the "emporium of fashion," where a lackadaisical milliner once a year fixes up the few bonnets that are worn or needed in this region of primitive tastes and accomplishments.

As far as the eye can reach, the surface is studded thick with "shafts" of the numerous mines with which these hill-sides are honeycombed. The lowest level worked is sixteen hundred feet. The quartz is brought to the surface and sold to the smelters, who are able to tell at a glance what any lot offered will yield. One of these mines which we visited was bought April first by its present owners, for one hundred thousand dollars. During April they took out twenty-nine thousand dollars. Fortunes are being made here, and changing hands, every month. The homes of the practical miners are unattractive, and there is little about the village to denote an advanced stage of civilization. Mining is not intellectually elevating in its tendencies, any more than digging wells or laying stone wall. Our party did considerable tramping, selected a few of the most brilliant specimens, tried to talk wisely to the natives, and were rather glad when the conductor announced that our train was ready. We made Denver at six o'clock, found an excellent supper at the station which detained us an hour, and at half-past ten were again in Manitou.

To-day, Sunday, our Connecticut party visited this place from which I date. Colorado Springs has a good assortment of churches. We came up here with the intention of worshiping at the Congregational establishment, but finding it late for service when we arrived, abandoned the intention. Everybody has heard of Colorado Springs, but not everybody knows there isn't a spring in the place; they are all at Manitou. But it is a very pretty and attractive village, though it has no springs. It has six thousand inhabitants, and its business is chiefly in cattle. It has a Catholic and an orthodox college, several stores, hotels, post-office, and a daily newspaper. Every western village has a daily newspaper. I don't know why some of them are printed, except it may be to keep up the price of white paper. Colorado Springs has several of those beautiful pink and salmon colored stone buildings which attracted my admiration at Denver. They tell me here the stone is not limestone or sandstone, but lava. I don't care by what name it is called; it is the finest building material in the world, with or without a name.

We shall spend Monday in Manitou, and leave Tuesday morning for a three days' trip among the mountains, taking in Marshall Pass, Leadville, and the La Veta Pass, expecting to arrive at El Moro on Thursday, May eighth.

IV.

Up Among and Over the Rockies—*Good Bye to Manitou—Royal George and Marshall Pass—The Snow Sheds—A Night at Sargent— Leadville on Both Sides — Veta Pass—Las Vegas Hot Springs—A Tribute to Raymond.*

In Transit, Near Santa Fe, N. M., May 9.

Four days and three nights in a narrow-gauge sleeping-car will occasionally test the good nature of as suave an individual as your humble servant. Our family of twenty in this particular car is composed of gentlemen and ladies in about equal numbers, with relations of kinship subsisting between but a portion of them. They all want to get up and dress at about the same moment in the morning; the dressing-room accommodations are adapted for but a single occupant at a time; and the average passenger feels obliged to wriggle into some sort of wearing apparel while yet in his berth, and before he appears even in the passage-way. That disrobing or enrobing, or observing the various conventionalities of polite society in these little toy houses on wheels, is with us or anybody a happy success, must be due to great good nature and forbearance on the part of all concerned. But I am glad to have had the experience, for while it has furnished additional evidence that " variety is the spice of life," it has also exhibited features in the funny side of railroading which none of us would now wish to have obliterated. Henceforward, from Santa Fé to the Pacific Coast, we travel on the broad-gauge Pullmans in which we left Boston.

My last letter was dated from Manitou, as our party was about leaving for its four days' excursion among the chief scenic wonders of the Colorado Rockies. Before leaving Manitou for good I cannot repress an allusion to the last half day spent there in visiting Williams Cañon and its ultimate attraction, the famous Cave of the Winds. The cañon itself is one of the most remarkable among the stupendous gorges of Colorado. The cavern is located three-quarters of a mile up this gorge, and its entrance is at the foot of a broad fissure in the cliff, perhaps three hundred feet above the trail. Registering our names, and paying each his admission fee of one dollar, the guide assisted us in donning loose outside garments, handed us lighted candles, and, under his lead, we proceeded up-stairs, down-stairs, through broad halls and wide chambers, and tortuous passages, upward of a mile into the bowels of the earth. Stalactites and stalagmites, in great profusion and beauty, met our admiring gaze in every direction. We stopped here and there to rest, and linger delightedly in the " bridal chamber," which is the acme of all and the holy of holies of this temple not made with hands. The guide cautions us to touch not, with appropriating hands, one of the least of the ten thousand stalactites which depend from the ceilings, or of the glistening and delicate fretwork which, in fantastic forms, adorns the walls of this brilliant chamber. When, however, we complete our explorations, and have returned to the welcome sunlight and purer atmosphere of the outside world, it astonishes us to find for how slight a recompense in coin of the realm the sordid cave-owner is induced to part with sundry specimens of the very things we had coveted while we roamed among them under the censorship of his hireling. We had not given the Williams Cañon and its cave much thought while selecting from among the attractions of Manitou's suburbs the objective points for our rides and tramps, and the brief visit here alluded to was in the best sense accidental. But let me say, in passing, that the tourist who bids good-bye to Manitou, having failed to take in the Cave of the Winds, makes a mistake forever to be regretted.

Tuesday morning we deposited ourselves in three of the cosiest of the cosy little sleepers of the Denver & Rio Grande Railway—narrow gauge—with an observation car attached, and started for El Moro, via the Royal Gorge, Marshall Pass, Leadville, and La Veta. That we might be unencumbered to the last degree, our trunks were forwarded, by express, direct to Santa Fé; the wisdom of which arrangement became increasingly apparent as we observed the small opportunity which these cars afforded for utilizing such luxuries as fresh linen or a change of head-gear. [I speak of capital adornment because that in my anxiety to appear well before the natives of Green Horn, Puker's Pass, and other metropole where our train might stop for refreshments, I took along my plug hat, one of Watrous's best, and new a day or two before leaving

Hartford. The very first night our admirable porter took pains to hang my tile on a hat-hook in such position that when he unshipped the upper bunk nearest it, the hat received an irreparable injury. I left it hanging upon a section post about three miles west of Salida, having taking the precaution to turn it inside out so that the maker's label might serve Watrous as an advertisement. As a consequence of this untimely episode I appear before the natives on dress parade in fatigue uniform, as plug hats are not to be had this side of San Francisco. The incident conveys a moral: Do not wear a stovepipe hat when you go West.]

The "Grand Cañon of the Arkansas," of which the supreme portion is known as Royal Gorge, extends ten miles above Cañon City. Its walls are high and precipitous, composed mainly of solid rock. Its principal features are similar to those of Williams Cañon, but infinitely more grand and imposing, and it has the added charm of a turbulent stream—the Arkansas River—tearing and tumbling among the boulders at the bottom of the gorge. The railroad, as at Clear Creek, follows the stream about fifty feet above its bed. At Royal Gorge, a bridge has actually been builded out from a projecting rock, supported by iron rafters in the form of an inverted V above it. The train is brought to a halt on this bridge, the party leave the cars and group themselves upon the causeway, where several stereoscopic views are taken, with the ledges in the background lifting their granite walls more than two thousand feet above. All through this cañon there are crevasses or rifts in the rocky sides, through which we catch bewitching glimpses of the Sange de Christo range of the Rockies, with Mount Ouray towering white and grand and beautiful, fourteen thousand and twenty-three feet above the level of the sea.

An easy run of an hour and a half brings

us to Salida, a place of some importance, and just now conspicuous on account of a recent discovery of gold and silver bearing leads in the hills one to three miles from the railroad station. The Salida mine is the most promising, specimens being shown us of ore from it which assayed five hundred and twenty dollars to the ton. The town was alive with strangers, evidently attracted thither by the new find. Salida has a population of about five thousand. All branches of trade seem to flourish there—particularly the gin business, it requiring fifty-three liquor shops and drug stores to supply the demand. With a few honorable exceptions the people appear to be of a vagabond class, living upon one another, and waiting for new contributions from outside to enable them to maintain the dignity and profit of their calling. And yet these wretches have the assurance to insist that there is nothing left of New England but a few decrepit old men and women, and to express their sympathy for our party as forlorn representatives of a section of country whose greatness has entirely departed! The best thing observed in Salida was the dinner served for us at the station dining-rooms.

At three forty-five P. M. we commenced the ascent of the spurs of Mount Ouray, on our way to Marshall Pass. This Pass is ten thousand seven hundred and twenty-five feet above the sea, and constitutes the dividing line between the Eastern and Pacific slopes of the Rocky Mountains. It is reached by a complex system of curves, the railroad doubling on itself no less than six times in making the ascent. As we advance up the mountain side the situation becomes grand and impressive beyond description. Hundreds of snow-covered peaks all about us come into clearer view above and below the fleecy clouds which toy and tremble and dissolve among the distant summits. As the train slowly creeps up the incline, new and deeper abysses constantly appal us on the one hand, while on the other the majestic heights scarcely diminish. We behold and wonder, and stand awed as if in the immediate presence of Omnipotence. We seem to be leaving things earthy, and advancing so surely toward the heavenly, that it is scarcely less than a disappointment when the train plunges into a cavernous snow-shed and the illusion is dispelled. But onward and upward the ponderous sixty-ton locomotive drags us, until, almost within hailing distance of the summit of Ouray, we come to a halt on the crest of the divide. This is Marshall Pass, almost eleven thousand feet above the sea, with perhaps a single exception the loftiest railway point in the world. The train waits here in the darkness a few minutes while the excursionists dismount and attempt to reconnoitre. I say "in the darkness," for you must bear in mind that at this point and all about us the snow is from ten to fifty feet deep; and Marshall Pass Station is a snow-shed nearly or quite a mile in length. On one side the shed abuts against the mountain; in the opposite side are occasional windows, which admit a few rays of light at intervals, and allow us another glance at the depths below or heights above and about us. We have obeyed the admonition of our conductor before reaching this great elevation, and stand in one another's presence in such mufflings and wrappings as each can command, and are not anxious to remain long outside the warm cars. A few of us step into the little telegraph office and interview the operator, who is a lady. She declines to accept the commiserations freely extended, and evidently considers her lot a happy one. She is forty and unmarried—which explains the situation. The railroad goes on over the Pass and down the west side of the mountain, this being the main line of connection with the Southern Pacific. We followed it as far as Sargent, where we took supper and lodgings. It is, perhaps, enough to record of this enterprising village, that none of its inhabitants went gunning among our party during the night, which good fortune on our part was at the time considered providential. It afterward transpired that an escaping horse-thief received their individual attention. We left Sargent Wednesday morning, retracing our way over the Pass to Salida, from which latter point we proceeded directly to Leadville, reaching that famous locality at three o'clock in the afternoon. The sixty miles between Salida and Leadville afford little of note. Occasional villages of a few hundred inhabitants put in an appearance, but they are all essentially alike; a few little one-story, dingy-yellow or wood-colored buildings, with now and then a more pretentious one; a few men loitering about in beggarly costume, with slouch hats, and pants stuffed in their boot-legs; a few burros meekly bearing their burdens; a few charcoal pits; and a few millions of acres of barren land surrounding; this will answer for a description of any or all of them. There is the magnificent mountain scenery all the time, and the delighful climate; the rest is poor enough.

But there is nothing monotonous or similar about Leadville. Leadville is unique. Let us be thankful for it. Perhaps I should remind you of its early history. The locality was first famous as "California Gulch," where, from 1859 to 1864, five million dollars of gold was washed out. The camp was afterward nearly abandoned, till during 1876 the discovery of carbonates was made, which led to a sudden influx of population. In February, 1878, the town of Leadville was organized, and two years later the city of the same name was incorporated with a population of fifteen thousand one hundred and eighty-five, of whom only three thousand seven hundred and forty-nine were females. This great carbonate camp of Colorado is said to be the richest mining district in the world. The product of bullion has increased from year to year, until in 1882 it exceeded eighteen million dollars. For a reason which I think will be apparent to a critical observer of its brief history, the population has gradually fallen off, until at present it is but about twelve thousand; and I suppose that the proportion of females is even smaller than when the census of 1880 was taken. The principal business institutions are six banks, fifteen smelting and reduction works, four foundries and machine shops, water works, gas works, lumber yards, stores, etc. There are three daily papers, schools, churches, hotels, etc. The number of mines within a radius of three miles of the city, is said to be upwards of two hundred, in many of which there are two and three relays of hands, so that work is kept up twenty-four hours of every day in the year. Leadville is ten thousand feet above the level of the sea, and the climate is absolutely unapproachable for salubrity and healthfulness. These are statistics which the historian naturally seeks, and such as you might expect me to collect and record during a brief tarry in the city.

You will fail of receiving a correct impression of Leadville, however, if I fail to make some further statements. And first in respect to gambling, which in its various forms is practiced there openly and by sanction of law. There are in this city of twelve thousand inhabitants upwards of thirty public gambling houses, which pay a revenue to the city of about one hundred thousand dollars per year. Every hotel has one, and some as many as six tables. The Board of Trade, which is a flourishing institution and owns its three-story brick block on the principal street of the city, is but a huge gaming house with all the modern appointments and conveniences. Its manager was formerly a resident of your city. I spent an hour at his office in very agreeable conversation relative to Hartford men and affairs. I visited one of the high-toned faro-banks at the corner of West Chestnut street, the proprietor of which is an alderman of the city, and was once a well-known citizen of Connecticut. At some other time I will give you their names. "Pap" Wyman, who used to drive his well-remembered four-horse silk wagon through Connecticut and Massachusetts, keeps a gambling resort and bar at the head of State street. He has an open quarto bible, well worn, on a handsome stand in a conspicuous place near the entrance; and above the bar, in bold gilt letters, is the legend "Please do not swear." The half dozen places which I visited were crowded with patrons. Everybody gambles; it is unquestionably the principal business of the city. Three men preside at every table and conduct the game. Of these one seems to be the dictator or referee. He occupies an elevated position above the others, and intently watches the movements of the cards and the disposition of the "chips." Young men and old were playing, some whose soft hands indicated that they were unused to manual labor, and many who were evidently just in from the mines. They surged in from the streets and waited for places at the tables; indeed there never seemed to be any cessation in the play.

In addition to these legalized gambling hells, the city has three variety theaters and any number of dance-halls. There are six hundred licensed prostitutes in the city, each of whom pays five dollars per month into the treasury. Vice in its worst and lowest and most repulsive forms not only stalks unrebuked, but is nursed and fostered as a chief source of public revenue. One of the city officials, who gave me this information, also assured me that the enormous city taxes of more than three cents on the dollar were actually reduced to but five or six mills by the revenue derived from licensed card tables, roulette tables, billiard tables, bars, theaters, saloons, dance-halls, and prostitutes!

Such is Leadville—the richest mining city in the world, but in its moral aspect decidedly the most degraded and hopeless. To one reared among the stern virtues of New England society, and the robust restraints of New England laws, the very atmosphere of Leadville seems to carry the taint of hell. No Sabbath, no God, the home a brothel, the chief inhabitants gamblers and prostitutes —what a place has the mammon of gold wrought out and set up to attract the young men of the east who would " make haste to be rich!" We shake the dust from our feet and leave Leadville under the friendly shelter of darkness. It is enough.

Thursday morning finds us back at Pueblo, one hundred and sixty miles from Leadville, at breakfast. At twelve we dine at La Veta, another hundred miles southwest, under the shadow of the foothills of the Sangre de Christo range. At two P. M. we are at Veta Pass, our ultimate destination on this supplementary trip. This pass, through which the Denver & Rio Grande Road gets over Dump Mountain at an elevation of nine thousand three hundred and forty feet, is scarcely less grand or beautiful in its scenic effects than Marshall Pass, already described, although at an altitude less by nearly one thousand five hundred feet. Some of the grades are actually heavier, its curves sharper, and its approaches more precipitous. In reaching its summit we travel fifteen miles from the valley, whereas to reach the summit of Marshall Pass we make a run of twenty-five miles from Salida, where the grade begins. None of this party will be likely to forget the delightful trip which occupied the afternoon of Thursday. The weather was perfect; every inch of the ride up the mountain was a panorama; the half hour at the summit was a picnic, and the tarry at La Veta on the return was a happy ending of a glorious day. I shall be derelict in duty if I fail to make acknowledgment of the efforts of our indefatigable manager, Mr. Raymond, to amuse and entertain his party at La Veta, whether by his pleasing performance on the little white burro, his violin concert at the La Veta Hotel, or as leader of the inimitable quartette at a later hour on the sleeper. These little incidents are of not much account to the outside world, but their mention will doubtless prove a pleasant reminder to the Raymond Party.

Friday morning we were aroused at five o'clock, to change cars at El Moro half an hour later. El Moro has three hundred and fifty coke ovens. The town takes its name (which signifies " The Castle") from the numerous rock elevations around it, each bearing striking resemblance to a castle or military fortification. We breakfasted at Raton, the border town of New Mexico, having now completed our journeyings in Colorado. Raton is noted as the railroad center of the coal-mining district of Colfax County. A thousand car-loads of coal can be produced and shipped daily from this point. Eighty miles southwest is Las Vegas, where we stopped for dinner. The city has nine thousand people. By favor of the railroad company we made a detour of five miles to the Las Vegas Hot Springs. There are thirty of them. The water has a temperature of one hundred to one hundred and fifty degrees. Its odor and taste are such as to indicate the presence of rotten eggs near the fountain-head. Its medicinal qualities are said to be wonderful. At Las Vegas we met an excursion party of somewhat more than a hundred, going East to Chicago and Boston, in six or seven Pullman cars. Our train pushes onward, past Levy, over Glorietta Mountain, at one time in sight of the ruins of an old Pecos Pueblo and church, and again under the frowning heights of Point Desolation, until Lamy is reached, eighteen miles from Santa Fé.

And here I bring this epistle to a close, in sight of the ancient city of whose quaint architecture and mixed population so much has been written. We shall remain at the Palace Hotel until Monday morning, and I hope in the interval to find material for an interesting letter.

V.

DESERTS, FLOWERS, ORANGE GROVES, VINE-
YARDS—*Santa Fé and its Adobes—The In-
dians of Arizona—A Thousand Miles of
Desert—Finally the Flowers and Oranges.*

LOS ANGELES, CAL., May 15th.

I closed my last letter to *The Post* just as we were about to enter the city of Santa Fé. There is so little to be said of this dull old town that perhaps I ought to have waited fifteen minutes and included the story of it in that letter; but since I did not, you will expect it now. The railroad station is a large half mile from the city. We traversed the distance in carriages—not on the backs of burros, the customary conveyance. It was a genuine novelty, this ride by moonlight through the narrow streets and among the adobe houses without any perceptible roofs, and into and across the swift-running river which courses through the heart of Santa Fé. For this river has only one or two narrow footbridges over it, and nowhere a bridge that can be crossed by a horse and carriage. The burros ford it, and the inhabitants who ride probably wouldn't get from one side to the other by any other process than fording it, if they had a dozen bridges. This is because their ancestors have done so. In Santa Fé, as in most other portions of New Mexico, the latest generation always imitates the preceding generation in all that is possible of imitation. Hence the mud huts, innocent of the commonest toilet conveniences; hence the filthiness of the surroundings of the habitations of the natives; hence the resemblance between the Santa Fé of 1542 and the Santa Fé of 1884.

This is the capital city of New Mexico. Its

population is about seven thousand, of which fully five thousand are Spanish and Mexicans speaking the Spanish language. It is the center of supplies for the surrounding country, and is constantly filled with freight wagons and pack animals. the latter being almost entirely the little burros or donkeys commonly used throughout the Territory. The supply of firewood for the city is almost wholly brought in on their backs. The valley is irrigated with water from Santa Fé Creek, it being well known by all authorities on the subject that no rain ever falls—although there were copious and drenching showers on both of the two days of our sojourn in the city. The climate is most agreeable, the atmosphere rare and pure, as might be expected at an altitude of seven thousand feet. The town is irregularly laid out, and the unpaved streets are narrow, crooked, and ancient-looking. The public square, or plaza, containing about two and a half acres, is bordered on three sides by the principal business houses, and on the fourth by the old "Palace," or Government building, containing the principal legislative chambers. The buildings are almost wholly of adobe, seldom more than one story in height. The adobe is simply mud, mixed with straw or stubble, formed in blocks eighteen inches long, nine inches wide, and four inches thick, baked by the sun until they are hard enough to be handled without breaking. Just outside each hut is a bake-oven, hemispherical in form, in which the family bread is baked during the day, and in which the family dog sleeps at night. I visited several of these huts, and, by the aid of an interpreter, succeeded in interviewing their inmates. Some of them are orderly and neat, as Mexican neatness goes, but they may be scented from afar every time. Within the town, and directly opposite the Palace Hotel—which is our home while in the city—is the military reservation of Fort Marcy. The stirring music of its military band woke our party to the realization of a serenade the first night after our arrival. On the heights north of the city are the ruins of old Fort Marcy, built and occupied by Kearney in 1846, when the Territory first fell under control of the United States. We visited the principal attractions of the city, namely, the old churches of San Miguel and Santa Guadaloupe, the exposition building, and the establishment where is manufactured the famous Mexican filigree jewelry. Some of our party took in an Indian dance at the Burro Exchange, while the rest of us remained at the Palace listening to Judge Sloan's taffy, and laughing at Almy's little story of the champion liar who was disemboweled by a panther, but survived by a neat transfusion trick. We parted from our friend and manager, Mr. Raymond, at Santa Fé, who placed us in charge of Mr. Harding from this point and returned to Boston to look after his White Mountain excursions. We reluctantly parted company, also, with Mr. Bradley of Worcester, who with his wife was summoned by telegraph to return on account of the death of his father. Sunday forenoon most of the party attended the Congregational Church, whose pastor is Rev. Mr. Kellogg, formerly of Jewett City, Conn. His pulpit was occupied in the afternoon by the venerable Dr. Worcester, a member of our party of excursionists. Monday morning we were breakfasted at six o'clock, and transferred from the hotel to the railroad station. The abominable chimes of the old cathedral rang out their matin as we entered the transfer carriages, bade farewell to the hospitable Palace Hotel, and were again put through Santa Fé Creek at its deepest ford in a style which would do credit to any Jehu, either east or west. We made the station safely, and at seven o'clock resumed our westward journey. The route took us back to Lamy, and thence southwest over the A., T. & S. F. Railroad. Sixty-seven miles away is Albuquerque, where we alight for a moment and greet another Connecticut man, Rev. Mr. Murphy, formerly of Granby and Essex, who is now pastor of a Congregational Church in Albuquerque. It seems remarkable, as it certainly is gratifying, to meet so many New England men at all important western localities; and we notice, too, that they generally hold positions of trust and influence. Just west of the place last named the train halts at a large Indian village to enable us to observe the natives. They come flocking about the cars, nearly or quite a hundred of them, with pottery and turquoises to sell. They are nearly all squaws, old and young, wearing none too much clothing for the weather, or for decency's sake. One little girl, perhaps ten years old, attracted my attention by her dress, which was that of civilization and unlike the garb of her companions. I ventured to address her, and found that she spoke excellent English. She had been three years at school at Albuquerque, and had learned to read and write as well as speak English with wonderful accuracy. In response to questions she told me her age and name, something about her home and associates, and soon became the central object of interest in our crowd. When asked why she dressed like little girls of civilized people, she promptly replied that since she had been to school she had no wish to follow the customs of her people in the matter of dress. It would have been a real pleasure if I could have made her a present of a suitable book, as she said she was fond of reading. But we had no other reading matter than the railroad time tables, so I was obliged to content myself with dropping a small coin into her hand, instead, for memory's sake.

For nearly two hundred miles, or as far as Rincon, we follow the course of the Rio Grande. Trees of respectable dimensions occasionally make their appearance, and some vegetation, in the way of stunted grass and the muskeet bean brush, makes it possible for immense flocks of sheep to nibble a good living. We took supper at Deming, and next morning started on the thousand-mile ride across the desert which lies west of the New Mexico and Arizona line. Drifting sands, and baked clay bottoms, and rocks, and sterile formations generally, succeed each other throughout the whole distance, varied only by occasional forests of cactus in every conceivable form of ungainliness, or growths of scrub cedar in spots where a little humidity make this low form of vegetable life possible.

There is very little worthy of note until long after we cross the Colorado River and get up into the vicinity of the San Bernardino Range of mountains. I should, however, make an exception of the repeated and wonderful mirages seen at several points on the desert, and especially just east of Tucson. No descriptions that I now recall of these strange illusions have conveyed to my mind any proper conception of the reality as beheld at the south of us during the Tuesday of our memorable trip across the sand plains of Central Arizona. At Benson Junction we passed the smelting works of the Tombstone Milling & Mining Company, whose stock is so largely owned in Hartford and other parts of Connecticut. The mines are twenty-two miles south. I am informed that the company is just now suffering from a strike among the miners, all work being suspended until the differences can be adjusted. The company pay three dollars per day; the miners want four dollars. At Tucson we meet the worst looking Indians yet seen—the Yumas—a bad lot, ugly, treacherous, repulsive to the last degree. Neither the "braves" nor the squaws have drapery enough about them to render their presence tolerable in the vicinity of a railroad station.

After running through one straight stretch of sand, sixty miles, we bring up at a perfect oasis—Dos Palmos—where are some elegant palm trees, and a variety of vegetation whose existence is accounted for by the fact that the soil was brought on cars and dumped there, and that is it kept irrigated from an artesian well close at hand. After leaving this breathing-spot we encounter but a few miles more of the desert, coming at Whitewater into the region of wild flowers, which delight and astonish us by their beauty and variety. From this place, on to Los Angeles, we find a succession of flowers in unnumbered millions, flowering cacti in all the shades of the rainbow, yucca blossoms in waxen clusters larger than the largest bunches of bananas, barley fields ready for the sickle, apricot orchards, orange groves yellow with fruit, acres upon acres of vineyards, the beautiful blooming alfalfa in its bed of green, and all the myriad forms of vegetation which is found only in this garden of the world. The contrast with the desolation of but an hour ago is so striking as to command the wonder and admiration of us all.

At Colton, fifty-eight miles from Los Angeles, where the train made a halt, I was surprised to observe upon the platform of the station your Mr. B. A. Simmons, the wholesale grocer of State Street. He is in the West looking after business interests, especially in the State of Arizona.

We reached Los Angeles at one o'clock this afternoon, and are housed at the Pico. A week is assigned for this beautiful region. Meanwhile the Yosemite parties will be made up, in which nearly every one of us expects to participate. Los Angeles has a population of over twenty thousand. Its main thoroughfares have an aspect of decided business activity. It is emphatically a city of groves and gardens. Fruits and flowers abound everywhere. There are large orchards and vineyards within the city limits, and many private residences are embowered in flowers and surrounded by park-like grounds. I have, of course, not yet had the opportunity for any very extended observations, but enough is already apparent to indicate numerous and inviting attractions for those who, like me, have known of southern California only by the books. I expect to visit Pasadena to-morrow, and all the other delightful suburbs on succeeding days. Oranges are ripe; if I can't get in a box of them for THE POST's editorial table, I may be able to ship you a few of the blossoms. We'll see.

VI.

DELIGHTFUL DAYS AT LOS ANGELES—*Some Surprises in the Valley—Sierra Madre Villa—The Groves and Vineyards—Great California Wineries—A Day at Santa Monica—The Climate.*

Los Angeles, Cal., May 18th.

I have spent four delightful days in this "City of the Angels." The city itself is very like a hundred other cities, in its streets, and buildings, and people, and business, and whatever else is likely to meet the eye of a casual observer. It has more Chinese and fewer Irishmen among its common people than has Hartford, for instance; but in all its material aspects it is not so unlike the average New England city of its size as to create any marked impression on the New England visitor who makes its acquaintance. It has picturesque hillsides on which nestle the cottages of the middle classes; so has Worcester, and so have scores of villages in our own State. Its broad avenues are bordered with the embowered palaces of wealth, with green lawns, and stately trees, and fountains, and singing birds; so are your Washington Street and Farmington Avenue, and as well the aristocratic streets and avenues of every other Northern city. It is not Los Angeles proper that impresses the stranger with a single pleasurable emotion that he has not already felt, perhaps, a thousand times. And this will account for the disappointment which manifested itself in the elongated countenances and sarcastic remarks of many of the Raymond Party the morning after the day of our arrival in the city. Some of them were actually sour. They thought they had seen it all, and were now ready to move on to San Francisco! Thursday's excursion in carriages dispelled the illusion, and taught us that the glory of Los Angeles is its suburbs. Let me describe our ride to Pasadena, San Gabriel, Sunny Slope, and the Sierra Madre Villa, a circuit of thirty-five miles entirely within the valley.

A right royal day it proved, in its favoring skies and the balminess of its atmosphere, but chiefly in the abundance of wonders which it brought to our amazed and now surfeited senses. The visual delights of landscape, and fruit, and flower, were a constant challenge to our highest admiration; the perfume of roses and orange groves made the thin air deliciously intoxicating; while the appeals to the palate which came from the orange orchards, the vineyards and the wineries, were entirely beyond our poor powers of resistance. To all these unfamiliar luxuries and temptations it must be confessed the majority of us became willing subjects. The valley, or succession of valleys, through which our route lies, is upward of a hundred miles in length, with an average width of about fifteen miles. It is watered by the Los Angeles River, from which hundreds of irrigating streams are diverted by means of canals, water-wheels, and hydraulic rams. For cultivation of the soil in all this part of the country the dependence upon artificial irrigation is absolute. Nothing is or can be produced without it. It is even more a feature here than fertilizing is in the East. This great valley, or such part of it as has been brought under cultivation, is covered with vineyards and orange orchards, with fields of barley, groves of lemon, fig, and English walnut trees. The roads are bordered with pepper trees, which at this season present a beautiful appearance, festooned as they are with their deep red clusters of ripening pepper berries. Palm and banana trees occasionally rear their graceful forms amid miles of cypress hedges, and the eucalyptus abounds everywhere, growing to great size and forming the chief dependence for fire wood. Groves of live-oak with its beautiful dark foliage fringe the streams and afford grateful shade upon the highways, the wild lands or occasional sand patches being carpeted with wild flowers in every conceivable hue, and in forms of wonderful beauty. The fig, the apricot, the peach, the Japanese plum, the olive, the pomegranate, and scores of other fruit-bearing trees with less familiar names, are all about us in fruit or bloom. Indeed, this drive of nearly forty miles affords a view of the fauna and flora of Southern California as complete as it is entrancing and memorable.

To me the chief objects of interest amid all this profusion are three, namely, the roses, the orange groves, and the vineyards. Of the first I can give you no adequate description. I have upon my table at this moment a bouquet of rose buds

which will average larger than a hen's egg.
I don't know their names, further than that
half of them are my special delight, the
moss rose. Others are white, salmon-colored,
the deepest red, and the loveliest blush.
The rose trees attain great size and are
most prolific. Some of the creepers are
trained to cover an entire arbor. I do not
think the roses are as fragrant as many
that we find East, but in magnitude of
bloom they rival the peony at its best. I
have seen several red roses that measure six
inches across. I should be greatly delighted
if a few of these Los Angeles roses could be
transplanted and made to thrive on certain
lawns which I could name on Winthrop
Street and Sigourney Street in your City of
Hartford.

Not everybody has seen an orange grove.
But everybody has an idea, from description
or otherwise, if he has not seen for himself,
how an orange grove looks. I had an idea,
but it was not the correct one. For instance,

I never saw or heard it stated that orange groves are plowed, and harrowed, and hoed, and kept as free from grass and weeds as a vegetable garden. But such is the fact; and when I saw my first " grove " standing on plowed ground, instead of on pasture land like the apple orchards of New England, I recorded the event as surprise number one. Again, while standing amid a cluster of orange trees and observing the profusion of great golden globes pendant from the branches in very direction, I ventured a remark to the gardener: "We are just at the proper season for seeing the fruit at its best?" "You may come again at Christmas, and it will be as you see it now," he replied. Which is true, for the orange tree of Southern California is ever green and ever bearing. It buds and flowers and fruits continually, from January to December. This was surprise number two. And while I am in the line of confession, it may as well be recorded here that my idea of a "grove" had by early education become so contracted that surprise number three awaited me when I rode straight through six miles of orange trees and learned that the plant extended miles on either hand. No name less dignified than "orange forests" will appropriately designate these great tracts of land devoted to orange culture in the Los Angeles Valley. The locality known as Pasadena is simply a great collection of private residences whose owners are orange growers. Their houses are palaces, and their grounds are flower gardens, each in the midst of an orange grove. There may be, but there need not be, a more beautiful spot upon earth. On the north of the valley, fifteen miles from Los Angeles, at the foot of the Sierra Madre Range of mountains, is the Sierra Madre Villa, a charming hostelry in the midst of an orange and lemon orchard, with an immense lawn covered with roses and tastily trimmed cypresses. We dined at the villa, and by courtesy of the proprietor went through the grounds and helped ourselves to fruits and flowers. The venerable doctor showed us every attention, making the brief visit exceedingly pleasant and profitable.

And now the vineyards. Grape culture is doubtless the principal industry of this portion of the State. The acreage under cultivation far exceeds that of the orange. There are twelve million grape-vines in the San Gabriel and San Bernardino Valleys alone. We passed on the road one vineyard of fifteen hundred acres, and scores of smaller ones covering anywhere from twenty acres up to many hundreds. We made a brief visit to L. J. Rose's famous ranche and vineyards, and to his winery. He owns five thousand acres of land, nine hundred and sixty acres of which are set with grapes, and six hundred acres with orange trees. The annual product of this winery is four hundred and fifty thousand gallons of wines, and eighty-five thousand gallons of grape brandy. Mr. Rose is owner of the famous trotting stallion "Sultan," which with several other noted horses were exhibited to us at the stables.

Through favor of Hon. Mr. Marx of Toledo, Ohio, a member of the party, your correspondent and the Messrs. Whidden of Boston were entertained at the great winery of Messrs. Kohler & Frohling, which is located near this city. This is not only the pioneer, but the most extensive wine house in the country. Its vineyards are here and in Sonoma, its warehouses in New York and San Francisco. Four thousand tons of grapes are crushed here annually, the product being seven hundred thousand gallons of wine, and thirty thousand gallons of brandy. This house has a national reputation for the excellence and purity of its wines, which are put upon the market in bulk, the casks being made upon the premises. We had the satisfaction of witnessing the various processes employed in wine making, and of testing the quality of the Angelica,

Muscatel, Port, and other brands produced here.

Friday was occupied by a few of us in a trip to Santa Monica, the alleged "Long Branch of the Pacific Coast." The Pacific Ocean is there—nothing more, if we except the lone fisherman who patiently, but unsuccessfully, waited for a bite during the four mortal hours that we tarried upon the sands. There are a thousand places on the Atlantic Coast between Portland and Charleston, either of which is more attractive as a seaside resort than Santa Monica. The place, however, affords a good sea-breeze, has a narrow beach with safe surf bathing, a bluff sixty or seventy feet high, and a little village a few rods back. It is the terminus of the Los Angeles & Independence Railroad, fifteen miles from the city. The ride to and from Santa Monica is very pleasant, the road passing through a highly cultivated section, as, indeed, may be said of the route by which every suburb of this objective point is reached.

In company with two other gentlemen I visited Washington Garden, a large park and orange grove in the western part of the city, Saturday. There is a pavilion and refreshment hall, with other facilities for enjoyment. Twenty-five cents gives the "freedom of the garden," which means to appropriate all the flowers and oranges one can eat or carry away in his pockets. I find that practice has raised my inside capacity to about ten, and that with overcoat and duster at hand I have pockets for about two dozen of the robust sizes. My room at the Pico Hotel has about a peck of orange blossoms, bestowed in various convenient places, which I have brought as trophies from one or another of the groves and gardens where this "freedom" has been extended. It is an uncommonly sweet room for a hotel—much sweeter then when first assigned to me.

After an experience of four days in Los Angeles I feel like confessing to considerable disappointment in regard to the climate. It has been represented as phenomenally salubrious and healthful. I have seen it stated repeatedly that the purity and dryness of its atmosphere are unequaled " elsewhere on the globe," and that it is particularly adapted as a residence for persons with weak lungs or of consumptive tendencies. I do not think that the facts warrant such statements. Each day has thus far been sunny, but there is a chill in the atmosphere, particularly in the early morning, which is very trying even to those whose lungs are not weak. Those of our party who have allowed their windows to remain open through the night, have almost without exception taken cold. I do not think the climate here is at all comparable with that of many places in Colorado. Sixty miles east, at Riverside, is a better place for invalids, because it is protected from the harsh ocean breezes and has a much more equable temperature. Los Angeles has obtained a good start, but Pomona and Riverside will give it a hard pull in the struggle for population and business.

They treat dead editors here with great respect. Thomas J. Caystile, late associate editor of the Los Angeles *Times* was buried this afternoon with very imposing ceremonies—bands of music, military, Knights Templar and Masonic organizations participating. Three thousand people were present. It was a great demonstration, and I have no doubt that among the deepest mourners of the editor dead was many a man who had "stopped his paper" on account of some fancied grievance from the editor living. Of the three daily papers published in this city, not one issues a Monday edition. They say the printers will not work Sunday!

Fifteen of our party started yesterday for the Yosemite; about as many more will go to-morrow, and another installment on Tuesday. The itinerary names Wednesday as the day of departure for those who go direct to San Francisco. That means your correspondent, among others.

VII.

TEHACHAPI PASS AND THE SIERRA NEVADAS —*Little Peculiarities of Los Angeles—Farewell Trips among the Orange Groves—The Mojave Desert—Crossing the Backbone—Approaching San Francisco.*

SAN FRANCISCO, CAL., May 23d.
We were a full week at Los Angeles; long enough to become familiar with everything except the wretched idiom of its Mexicans and "greasers," and the insoluble intricacies of Los Angeles veracity. I have known some accomplished prevaricators in the land of steady habits, but none whose exploits deserve record in the distinguished category where the inhabitants of this city appear. Falsehood floats serenely in the atmosphere of the real estate offices, impedes your pro-

gress in shopping tours among the merchants, and drops in chunks from the bland countenance of the heathen Chinee as he returns five of your twelve pieces from the laundry and swears "him alle here." We left at half past seven oclock A. M., although the time-table had it quarter past twelve, and our native porter insisted that the train would depart at high noon. Divers of our party have been apprehensive of possible infection during the protracted period of our sojourn in the city. As you will observe, however, by this paragraph, no indication of taint has yet made it appearance among us.

Despite the little impediment above alluded to in the way of our highest enjoyment of local society, I think it may be said truthfully (not according to the Los Angeles standard) that the week has been pleasantly and profitably spent. I have in a previous letter given you some account of visits to several suburbs of the city. These visitations were continued, including pretty much every locality of interest within a radius of a dozen miles. Through the continued and abiding courtesy of my friend Whidden of Boston, I was entertained during one eventful day at the magnificent villa and orange ranch of Mr. James Ford, ten years ago a resident of the old Bay State, and a personal friend of your Boston correspondent, Hon. B. P. Shillaber, from whom Mr. Whidden carried letters of introduction. Mr. Ford's place lies under the shadow of the Sierra Madre Range. His ranch contains fifty acres under cultivation, being principally orange grove and vineyard. The approach to his charming residence is through a private avenue bordered with orange trees, in full fruit, more than half a mile in length and leading in a straight line from the highway to the plaza upon which the cottage stands. We were received with royal hospitality by the proprietor and the ladies of the family, who in many graceful ways facilitated our participation in the wealth of fruits and flowers by which they are surrounded. I do not need to say that the occasion was one of great and lasting interest.

My farewell suburban ride and walk, still in the company of the friend above mentioned, was to the largest orange orchard in the world, a short distance west of Los Angeles. It is owned by a Mr. Wolfskill, who puts upon the market this season twenty-five thousand boxes of oranges and five thousand boxes of lemons. It is an immense affair. The grounds are patrolled by an Englishman with half a dozen dogs, whose business it is to intercept intruders. Although our party were provided with a permit from headquarters, this officious English dignitary, with an obtuseness of intellect which has characterized his ancestry since the days of George III., was inclined to dispute our progress. We finally succeeded in convincing him that we were not tramps, or thieves, or escaped convicts, and passed on unshot by him or "unchawed" by his dogs. Mr. Wolfskill has a great bonanza in his orange orchard. He gets three dollars a box for the fruit.

I had a very pleasant interview Tuesday evening with Mr. F. O. Mosebach, formerly of Hartford, who is a practicing attorney in this city, and who also has the general agency here for the Hartford Fire Insurance Company. Mr. Mosebach was for several years in the investment department of the Ætna Life at the home office. He came here from Hartford somewhat less than two years ago. His professional business here is quite large, and he is the owner of a ranch of one hundred and sixty acres, about forty miles north of the city. He is an accomplished gentleman, and it is a pleasure to record his prosperity.

Our final departure for San Francisco was delayed eighteen hours by a railroad disaster near Deming, which prevented the Pacific express from getting through until the morning of the twenty-second. The unpleasantness of this delay was fully compensated, however, by the daylight trip which it secured for us over the Tehachapi Summit and through the pass of the same name amid the Sierra Nevada Mountains—a part of the route invariably passed over in the night time when trains run by schedule either way. The distance from Los Angeles to San Francisco is precisely four hundred and eighty-two miles. Thirty-six miles from the first-named city, at an altitude of about one thousand five hundred feet, the famous San Fernando Tunnel, more than a mile and a quarter in length, passes through the mountain of the same name. Then we enter the Mojave Desert, and travel a full hundred miles through a scene of wilderness and desolation, save only for the abundant wild flowers which spring everywhere from the unwatered sand. Forests of cactus of course abound in all their ugliness, and sage brush occasionally relieves the bareness of the surface. But for hours this monotony of desert scenery is unbroken by any evidence of civilization, while the lizard and ground-squirrel appear to be the sole representatives of animal life in all the dreary waste. By gradual ascent, however, the summit before alluded to is reached, and then we begin the wonderful and seemingly perilous ride down the northern slope. For twenty-four miles we descend over an average grade of one hundred and sixty feet to the mile, through seventeen successive tunnels, each from three hundred to a thousand feet in length, winding among the mountain tops and over yawning chasms upon frail trestle-work, the railway once actually crossing its own path where a drop of a hundred feet could be accomplished in no other way. From some of these altitudes the scenery is surpassingly beautiful. We look down upon a thousand lower heights, as one looks from the top of Mount Washington upon the summits which lie below it; while in a hundred distant valleys, and upon the slopes of as many hillsides, the dark and dense foliage of clustering live-oaks appears in charming relief against the lighter green and brighter colors of alfalfa and wild flowers and barley fields which carpet the earth as far as the eye can see in the direction of the broad valleys of the San Joaquin and the Sacramento. The transition from desert on the south to almost tropical verdure on the north of this "backbone of the continent" is exceedingly impressive, accomplished as it is within a few moments of time, or simply by traversing the less than half a mile of level ridge which constitutes the "Divide." It is said, and doubtless truly, that this twenty-four miles of way up and down and among the Sierra Nevadas is the most remarkable triumph of railroad engineering skill ever achieved in any part of the world. An employé on the train informed me that three civil engineers of great repute first undertook to survey a passage through these peaks and crags, and after repeated attempts declared a route impossible of location. A boy of twenty took up the job where his elders had forsaken it, and this miraculous Pass is the result. It must have cost a vast deal of money as well as of brains, and it is doubtful if the undertaking ever could have become a success except with the aid of government appropriations and the cheap labor of the Chinese. I remember with grand satisfaction my experiences at Marshall and Veta Passes, at Clear Creek Cañon and the Royal Gorge, and among the other wonders of the Colorado Rockies; but I think the impressions received in the descent from Tehachapi Summit will be quite as lasting, and infinitely more of a "joy forever" than either of the wonderful works of nature or art which has taken precedence with me in the order of its beholding.

Night overtook us soon after leaving Sumner Station,—a locality which will be remembered chiefly by reason of the luxurious supper which was provided there for our delectation. Tipton and Toulare were successively reached in good order, though it must be confessed that neither received from myself or my friend Whidden the attention which may have been their due. This possible dereliction in duty on the part of your correspondent, should you think best to require an explanation, is accounted for by the demands which Talbot and Knowlton were at that time making upon us in an undecided game at whist. The fertile valley of the San Joaquin, with its one hundred and fifty miles of continuous wheat fields, would have been at least worth looking at, but there was no moon and the occupants of the train were honestly attempting to get asleep, after being roused at Madera by the misguided portion of our party who insisted on being let off there to make a midnight start for the Yosemite. At half-past four in the morning the irrepressible porter announced that we were approaching Oakland, and must dress immediately in order to catch the ferryboat for San Francisco. Everybody obeyed promptly. The train passing a station about ten minutes later, time tables were consulted and Oakland found to be more than forty miles away. I sat down in an easy corner and tried to woo sleep. The sun was just showing itself in the east. A voluble gentleman came in from a rear Pullman and sat down beside me. He had been in San Francisco once before, and of course knew every object about us at a glance. He called the names and pointed out the localities of all the villages through or in sight of which we passed, and voiced the remarkable pronunciations with wonderful facility. This was "San Hosay," and that was "Mairsade," and the other was "Velayo," and so on, far and near. He filled me up with statistics, and explained the reason why "we" raised "only" two hundred and thirty thousand tons of wheat in the "San Waukin" valley last·year. In process of time we reached Oakland, and the train halted at the upper station; but the gentleman talked on, and called my attention to the Golden Gate, and was still on the *qui vive* for something new to do or say for my delectation, nor gave himself a thought, until as the train was moving on the conductor passed us and dropped to the loquacious stranger a remark: "I thought you wanted to get off at Sixteenth street." This was Sixteenth street. The man got off at Sixteenth street, but in a demoralized condition owing to the headway of the train. If I had not become very tired of his well-intended attention, too tired to exert myself, I should have made an effort to repress the smile which stole over me as he gathered himself and beat the soil from his pants and settled his hat firmly in place. It was rude for me to smile, but I know my rudeness was not observed by him.

We reached San Francisco at seven o'clock

this morning, and proceeded at once to the Palace Hotel, from which I now write. Half the time allotted for the entire trip has now been consumed, though we have but just reached the extreme western terminus. We shall remain in this city two full weeks, spend four days in Monterey, leaving for the East on the eleventh of June. I will reserve for another letter whatever is to be said of San Francisco and its surroundings, which we shall have ample time and opportunity to observe. Up to the present time our party have been wonderfully favored with good weather, good health, and freedom from delays and other vexations of travel. I think the management of Mr. Raymond and his successor, Mr. Harding, has been wise and eminently satisfactory. So far as has been possible, all our wants have been promptly provided for, and our highest comfort promoted. I am reminded to say this now, because of the very different experiences of other parties with whom I happen to have come in contact en route, and not with a desire to pat anybody's back.

P. S.—I quite unexpectedly met our mutual friend M. Bennett, Jr., in the dining hall at the Palace an hour ago. It was a most agreeable surprise.

VIII.

The California of '49 and '84—*The Topography of San Francisco—Cable Cars—The Palace Hotel—A Drive Among the Suburbs—Sunday—The Chinese Quarter—An Opium Den—Disgusting Situations.*

San Francisco, Cal., May 28th.

I find it difficult to realize that this great, bustling city is the California of '49. We old fellows who were boys when the gold fever broke out, who still remember how our older acquaintances of that remote period embarked on the seven-months' trip "'round the Horn," in search of the far-off land of gold, have always been in the habit of thinking of California as a great mining camp, where the chief industry is, and ought to be, digging for gold. And so, when I come to San Francisco and find it a commercial city like Boston, and hear people say that all there is of interest to tourists in California is to be found right here, ignoring the old memories, and the old experiences, and all that, it seems to me as if there must be something wrong somewhere. I want to get back into the gulches and among the foot hills, and dig a little myself. It seems as if there should be a good many nuggets in California yet, for they don't pretend to claim that the State has been more than half dug over by squatters and prospectors. Whatever the present situation, as regards the importance of mining interests in this State, it is certain that San Francisco was born of the gold excitement of 1848 and 1849. First a place of rendezvous for fortune seekers, it became successively a depot of supplies, a wideawake and populous town, and on through advancing stages until, as before stated, its inhabitants now affirm that it embodies all there is of consequence in the whole state. But let me start again and tell you something of the city as I have observed it.

The topography of San Francisco will be well represented in miniature, if you place two soup tureens and five bowls bottom up on your dining table, and throw a table cloth loosely over the whole. If your table be oblong, let it stand lengthwise east and west, and let the tureens be placed side by side, each pointing across it; the bowls may flank the other dishes at their outsides. These seven elevations and the surrounding surface will very well represent the seven hills and surrounding plain on which the city is situated. If you add a particularly deep bowl near the northeast edge, to represent Telegraph Hill, the topographic illusion will be complete. Some of the longest and most important streets, like California and Geary Streets, run in a straight line from the east edge of the table, outside which is the bay of San Francisco, over the soup tureens and bowls to the western edge, which is the Pacific Ocean. Many of these hills are so steep that no vehicle, except the cable cars, can go up or down them, and the grass, therefore, literally grows in the streets. And, by the way, these cable cars are the very perfection of street railway service. Each car is one half open and the other half closed. No matter how heavy the load, they go right up and down the steep hills and across the plains at a uniform rate of speed, always under the instant control of the "driver." No baulky horses, no carrying the passenger half a dozen blocks out of his way because the car cannot be stopped on an up grade, none of the whipping and swearing and confusion which signalize the transit up your Asylum Hill, but the simple shifting of a lever and off she scoots over tureens and bowls two hundred feet high, without the slightest apparent effort. From the Palace Hotel these cable cars run momently to every part of the city, and connect with steam cars and steam ferries to all the important suburbs. The route through California Street passes over the summit of Knob Hill, where are located the elegant residences of ex-Governor Stanford, General Colton, Hon. Charles Crocker, Mrs. Mark Hopkins, Flood, O'Brien, and the other millionaires whose names are familar in political and commercial circles. Their grounds are charmingly laid out and cultivated with exquisite taste. The residences of all classes throughout the city are almost uniformly of wood, with a tendency to jig-saw ornamentation which is so universal as to excite unfavorable criticism. Stone and iron, and brick faced with mastic, are used with good effect in the construction of the most imposing edifices in the business part of the city. I suppose that this Palace Hotel, at which the Raymond Party are quartered, is one of the chief wonders of San Francisco. It is the largest hotel in the world, as well as the richest and most elegant. It covers an area of ninety-six thousand two hundred and fifty square feet, and the distance around it is exactly one-quarter of a mile. There is a promenade on the roof of one-third of a mile. The grand central court, into which the visitor in his carriage is first ushered, is about one hundred by one hundred and fifty feet, seven stories high and roofed with glass. Ornamental balconies run around its four sides, at each floor, on which are growing tropical plants and flowering shrubs, making the place one of rare beauty and attractiveness. Around the ground promenade are grouped the office, reception parlors, reading-rooms, breakfast and dining-rooms, etc., with spacious communicating hallways. The rooms are mostly *en suite*, very large, and handsomely furnished at a cost of more than half a million. The structure itself cost six millions. Its exterior is also very elegant, every window being a bay window on both the Market and Montgomery Street fronts. Ex-Senator Sharon is the owner of the property, and it is under the management of his nephew, Alexander D. Sharon. There is a great number of very fine stores on Market Street and its tributary thoroughfares, representing as wide a range of trade as can be found in Eastern cities. Andrew's diamond palace on Montgomery Street, and some others that I have noticed, may be classed with the most pretentious of their kind in New York or Boston.

A carriage drive through Golden Gate Park, past the cemeteries, and on toward Point Lobos and its famous Seal Rocks, has familiarized me with about all there is between the bay and the ocean worth mentioning. Nobody who comes to San Francisco fails of visiting the Seal Rocks, or rather the beach and Cliff House, close by which the rocks are seen. This point on the Pacific Coast may be called the Coney Island of California—that is, if we grant to Santa Monica the other title, which she has appropriated, of the "Long Branch of the Pacific." At the northern terminus of a long sandy beach rises a rocky bluff; and where the rock rises highest and almost overhangs the ocean, at an altitude of a hundred feet or more above it, they have built a handsome hotel which is called the Cliff House. From its broad and sheltered verandas there is an unobstructed view of the coast for a great distance, while on the west the blue expanse of the Pacific extends away to the horizon. From three hundred to five hundred feet seaward of this Cliff House, and washed continually by the surging waves which break under its very foundations, are two groups of rocks, which have given the place its celebrity. These rocks are five in number: the highest and largest reaches an elevation of perhaps eighty feet at low tide; the smallest is barely seen above the surface at high water. The largest displaces a circular area of water perhaps one hundred and twenty feet in diameter; the smallest is about as large as an old-fashioned country school-house. These rocks are the resort of hundreds of seals, which swarm and wriggle and squirm over them continually. The first sight of them at a little distance was most disgusting, each individual rock strongly reminding one of an immense fragment of cheese filled with squirming black maggots. The water seemed to be alive with these seals. They are most expert swimmers, and are constantly climbing out of the water upon the rocks, or tumbling off from the rocks into the sea. It is very amusing to watch them, buffetted by the waves, in their patient efforts to get a foothold on the slippery rocks, and then in their awkward climbings upward and over the ledges. By the aid of a glass I could observe them quite critically. They grow to great size, and the largest appeared fairly gray with age. I understand they attain a weight of a thousand pounds, though none of those I saw upon the rocks looked as if they weighed much more than half that, and the average seemed to be perhaps one or two hundred. The small ones were playful, and kept up an incessant barking; but the old fellows evidently preferred to lie quietly in the sunshine, for they would occasionally make things very unpleasant in their neighborhood when disturbed or approached by others more actively inclined. I sat on the veranda of the Cliff House for a couple of hours in the interested observance of this strange and constantly changing picture. There is an unaccountable fascination about it, as I understand, for everybody who comes here. This beach, and the three or four hotels thereon, with the Seal Rocks, constitute a sufficient attraction to draw about two hundred thousand visitors hither every year.

Sunday morning I attended service at the Howard Presbyterian Church on Mission Street, of which Dr. McKenzie is pastor.

Being now absent on his vacation, his pulpit is supplied by Dr. Stratton, President of the University of the Pacific, a Methodist Theological Institution. He ranks among the most eloquent pulpit orators of the State. In the afternoon I accidentally heard part of a harangue from the female exhorter of a salvation army which paraded the streets with drums and banners. Still later in the afternoon, strolling in the vicinity of the City Hall, I was attracted by the brogue of an Irishman who was talking to an audience of a hundred or two men and boys. Seeking information of the orator from a passing policeman, I found that it was Dennis Kearney, he of the "sand lots." Of course his theme was politics. I have been surprised to find so much regard paid to the proprieties of the Sabbath here. There certainly is less profanation of holy time in San Francisco than in Chicago; a more general suspension of business, and a more decorous manner of action and speech from those who walk the pavement or lounge at places of common resort. I should feel some surprise, too, in seeing the women on the streets daily in sealskin dolmans and fur-lined cloaks, and the men in heavy overcoats, so near the first of June, if the chilly trade-winds didn't cause me to forget the proximity of the summer solstice in my longings for the substantial winter wraps which I left in Hartford. I do not like the climate of San Francisco, or its winds.

And there is one other feature which I must not omit—the Chinese. I made the tour of Chinatown last evening, in company with five other gentlemen and under the protection of a well-known guide. Let me give you the names of these gentlemen, for whatever of ignominy or renown attaches to the tour, I feel that it should be shared by us individually. There was Mr. Almy for the heavy weight, Mr. Merriam as legal adviser, Mr. Craven and Mr. Bull, who were selected on account of their good looks, while Mr. Richards and myself were there to uphold the dignity of the occasion. Detective Jackson intended a compliment when he remarked at the outset that there was no probability of our becoming any worse for what he was about to show us! I think we saw something of every phase of Chinese life. The Chinese Quarter is included within eight blocks—four in length by two wide. It is in the heart of the city. Forty thousand Chinamen and women occupy these eight blocks. Of course they are packed like sardines. We visited their money and stock exchange, their provision markets, drug stores, shops, and warehouses. We watched their native barber as he scraped the unlathered face of his customer, sitting bolt upright on a stool. With a long, narrow, flexible blade, the artist mowed over every square inch of surface from his breast-bone to the back of his head, digging out his ears and nostrils, scraping with equal care the bridge of his nose, his forehead, and every other spot, whether encumbered with beard or not. We drank tea and ate native refreshments at Chin Lang Pin's high-toned restaurant, saw all the nonsense of the Joss House, and brought away therefrom sundry souvenirs in the shape of ready-made prayers, joss sticks, and other tomfoolery. Every worshipper at this institution is obliged to pay something, and this is the novel method of assessment: The boss of the place has a number of smooth sticks about a foot long, on one end of each of which is a character representing a sum of money. He places these sticks in a large wooden spoon-holder, lettered end inside, gives the spoon-holder a shake and passes it around. Each worshipper picks out his little stick and pays the sum indicated on it. The plan seems to afford complete satisfaction, each Pigtail giving a grunt and smiling a smile which appears to indicate that he thinks he has got off a little easier than his neighbor. It cost our crowd four bits to get away with this part of the entertainment. We went through the places where these people live. The houses are not high, none over three stories above ground, but they go down indefinitely into the bowels of the earth, and the deeper and darker and more contracted and airless the place, the better the occupants seem to be pleased. The rooms average about six feet square; the largest are perhaps eight by ten feet, and there are many below the average. The rooms have almost no furniture. A house will contain, between its lowest sub-cellar and roof, from one hundred to five hundred of these rooms, and it is a pretty lonesome room that has not five or six Chinamen in it when they are all at home. Thus you see it is not very difficult to account for the five thousand people who occupy each of the eight blocks of the Chinese Quarter.

But it is in the opium dens that they pack them away thickest. These run two and three stories underground, and seem to extend pretty much through the entire colony. An opium den contains perhaps thirty rooms or cells ranged around a long and narrow court. Each cell has tiers of bunks just wide, long, and high enough to accommodate the prostrate form of a man. Each is furnished with a piece of matting, a filthy pillow about ten inches square, a small lamp, and an opium pipe which looks like a flute without any keys and with a porcelain door-knob attached near one end. The door-knob part contains the opium, which the smoker melts and manipulates until it reaches the proper condition, when he sticks the small end of the flute into his mouth, ignites the drug, sucks and swallows and gasps alternately, until he finally passes off into a state of apparent stupefaction, and the attendant comes and removes the pipe and lamp. The bunks, with pipes and other paraphernalia, are rented by the proprietor of the place, and there appears to be no lack of patrons. We explored but one of these dens, and that was quite full. The cells and alleys were like dungeons, dark, filthy, thick with opium smoke, and absolutely unventilated. I do not understand how the inmates manage to sustain life there. I was well nigh suffocated simply in transit.

I don't know whether the Chinese, as a class, in this city are more vicious than other nationalities. We saw a great many tableaux vivant representing every conceivable variety of evil; but then, our guide was instructed to show us Chinatown, and he obeyed orders without restrictions. I suppose that an exploration in other quarters, among French, Spanish, Mexican, or even American people, might reveal equally shocking and disgusting situations. For some reason there seems to be a cordial dislike of the Chinese by all other nationalities here, yet I do not see how San Francisco could get along without them. They do all the menial work, the drudgery of domes-

tic and business life, and they do it well
and cheaply. They are industrious, orderly,
mind their own business, and are honest as
honesty goes among the masses. I could
name a race of people among us for whom,
in my opinion, it will be less tolerable in
the day of judgment than for the heathen
Chinee.

IX.

THE SUNDRIES OF SAN FRANCISCO—*Memorial Day—The Cemeteries—Some Noted Mausoleums—Floral Wonders—California Journalism—The Sharon Racket—A Chinese Funeral—Sunday Evening on the Street.*

SAN FRANCISCO, CAL., June 1st.
Memorial Day, recurring during my stay in this city, has afforded an unanticipated opportunity of witnessing several quite admirable displays. First, of the people in holiday attire, pouring out to observe or participate in the ceremonies of honoring the patriotic dead; next, the military display, including a parade of several regiments of the volunteer militia, detachments of the Grand Army, veterans of the last war, and "Sons of Veterans" of the war of the

Revolution, the war of 1812, and the Mexican war; and last, though chief in attractiveness to me, the great wealth of flowers contributed for the service, such as probably no other city in the country could produce. The military pageant was easily witnessed from the Market Street balconies of the Palace Hotel, headquarters of the commanders having been established here, and the line forming on the streets centering at this point. The immense court of the hotel was filled with distinguished visitors, and the seven tiers of balconies above with ladies and gentlemen, while the military band in the courtyard rehearsed dirges and marches until ten o'clock, when the great procession moved. The line of march was not long, and when Van Ness Avenue was reached the military were disbanded, the Grand Army boys proceeding directly to the cemeteries by the cable cars on Geary, Haight, and California Streets, followed by wagon-loads of flowers in various designs, as well as loose. Among the designs I noticed an immense mounted cannon composed entirely of great white calla lilies; a square shaft ten feet high and of proportionate size, made up of monster white carnations, with a wreath of pansies inlaid upon each of the four sides, and a cluster of golden buds, which I did not recognize, at the apex; a brace of cavalry swords crossed, made of solid lilies of the valley, with their golden handles and guards formed of velvety dwarf marigolds, the whole resting on a bank of royal purple pansies, studded with little stars of orange blossoms, which were charmingly shaded down to the purple by a peculiar arrangement of mignonette. Some of the heavy designs, like shields and anchors, were made up of solid rose-buds in grades of size and shade which would be altogether impossible except in a region of roses like this. There were cut flowers in bouquet and loose, which I cannot name, and in profusion which required altogether several large teams to move them to the cemeteries.

About three miles from this hotel, near the western limit of the city, stands "Lone Mountain,"—a bold, bare eminence perhaps six hundred feet above the surrounding level. Upon its summit, which can be seen from all directions for many miles, has been erected an immense cross, which has no significance except to indicate that the ownership vests in the holy Catholic Church. The burial grounds of the city cluster about this mountain. They are five in number, and all quite large. As I have perhaps made sufficient allusion to these in a previous letter, I will only say here that the various grounds had, during the preceding two or three days, been trimmed up and otherwise placed in a state of preparation for these services, and that they presented a more attractive appearance than when I saw them the preceding Sunday. The Catholic Cemetery contains the best as well as the poorest monuments. In it is the magnificent mausoleum of the millionaire O'Brien, costing over one hundred and fifty thousand dollars; also the Sharon monument and enclosure, together with a score or more of chapels, monuments, and shrines, which are very beautiful and very costly. Amid all and everywhere are the always abounding and ever blooming floral wonders which make beautiful alike the poorest sepulchres of the common herd and the silent palaces of the princely dead. I see by the papers that over three thousand bouquets and floral designs were contributed and placed upon soldiers' graves in the various cemeteries during the impressive ceremonies of Friday. It was such an offering as could be made by no other city in the land.

We have now been in San Francisco considerably more than a week, and have probably seen pretty much everything of interest here. I have visited the beautiful Golden Gate Park no less than three times, and have found in its conservatory, or elsewhere, each time increased reason for admiration. It is magnificent in the variety and extent of its surface and scenery, and in the perfection of its appointments. The old church of the Dolores Mission, three hundred years old, is an object of considerable curiosity. So is the new City Hall, which has been in course of construction for many years, and is yet unfinished because of lack of funds. And the Jesuit College, and the Pavilion, and the Mint—and the whole city. Van Ness Avenue is the finest street, and the "Western Addition" the finest section of the city. One of the prettiest drives is through the Park and

"Over the hills to the poor-house,"

winding as it does among the foot-hills of "The Twin Peaks," and upon various commanding eminences. Inspiration Point, just south of the Mission, is the most advantageous position for a general view of the city and the bay. I saw a gang of twenty men and boys digging potatoes on the premises of the alms-house a day or two since. It is the first time I have seen potatoes harvested in May.

Members of our party who went into the Yosemite Valley are now arriving at the Palace. They represent the roads as very bad, and the snow so deep as to have prevented their visiting some desired points, particularly the big tree where it is said a stage can be driven through a cavity in the trunk. But the scenery generally is the same in grandeur and sublimity that it has so often been pictured. The trip into and out of the valley was attended with much hardship and hazard, and individual members of the party will carry weary limbs and "cricky" sides for some days yet. But I do not hear that anybody regrets the experience.

You may be interested to learn what are my impressions of San Francisco journalism. As you already know, there are six daily papers in the city, four morning and two evening. The morning papers also print Sunday editions. In circulation and influence the dailies all appear to be on an excellent footing, and they easily hold the field against all attempted competition. *The Chronicle* occupies a leading position among its contemporaries, *The Call, The Alta, The Examiner, The Post,* and *The Bulletin,* following in about the order indicated. The first two and last two are Republican in politics, *The Examiner* Democratic, and *The Alta* " independent "—that is, reserving the privilege of leaning toward the side which can offer strongest inducements. The dailies publish double sheets on Sunday, and also on Tuesday—though why Tuesday any more than any other secular day I have not been able to discover. It is a noticeable feature of San Francisco journalism that the papers by common consent go ahead and print the news, leaving the bickerings and bitterness and brag for somebody else to indulge in. There is less personality in *The Chronicle*, for instance, than one would expect to find in a journal of its scope, and especially when the nationality and characteristics of its proprietor are taken into consideration. I have heard no estimate of the respective circulation of these papers, further than that, after *The Chronicle*, they print editions not widely apart in numbers. There is an English-speaking population of more than two hundred thousand in San Francisco, which fact alone warrants the belief that the apparent prosperity of these six dailies is also real and permanent. I notice that while advertising is extensively done in all the papers, scarcely any large and black type is used. As a consequence, the papers have a neat and handsome appearance, and the general effect is really to render all advertisements more attractive than they could be amid a wilderness of cuts and heavy display lines. San Francisco may be said to be thoroughly metropolitan in its newspapers; it produces as good as the best.

And this leads me to speak of the disgraceful " Sharon *vs.* Sharon " trial now occupying the attention of the superior court in this city, and which furnishes the papers with three or four columns of sensational reading every day. The suit is brought by a Miss Hill for breach of alleged promise of marriage. Sharon, the defendant, is sixty years old, a widower, and by his own confession a libertine of the most accomplished sort. The situation divulged by evidence is simply infamous. But Sharon is rich in uncounted millions, and I suppose the woman thinks she can get most money through the courts. She evidently has no modesty to be shocked by the appalling disclosures of her paramour. San Francisco's history abounds in kindred episodes, which are within the memory of all of us. Among them this Sharon scandal will scarcely remain a seven-days' wonder.

I have attended divine service to-day at the church of Dr. Stone—formerly of Middletown, Conn., as I perhaps do not need to remind you. The doctor is very old and rarely officiates. His colleague, Dr. Barrows, is away on his vacation, and we listened to a stranger. This is the finest church edifice in the city and as near perfection in its interior arrangement as any audience room I have ever seen. There have been two military funerals here to-day, the first largely attended by military men and conducted with quite imposing ceremonies. A Chinese funeral was also solemnized this morning. It consisted, so far as public demonstration was concerned, in one wagon-load of corpse and two wagon-loads of refreshments for ditto. The refreshments were principally baked meats, among which what looked like roast goose and roast pig were prominent. The mourners were conspicuous by their absence. A Chinese menial at the Palace tells me that the mourning is all done at the Joss House. The relatives take no active part in that. The same menial volunteers further information to the effect that the souls of Chinamen all have to go to heaven by way of China; that it takes about two years to reach their destination by that route, and that they require to be well fed on the journey. Hence the funeral baked meats and the goose and the succulent pig.

It is Sunday evening and nearly nine o'clock as I write this paragraph. Yet it is not the New England Sunday. The din which comes to my ears from the street makes me feel as if I ought to get out and see the circus coming into town. But it isn't the circus. It is only the orchestra on the balcony of the Market Street Theater, a block away; and the gang of hoodlums with the drums are merely stray waifs from the tarflats who have unconsciously wandered outside the bailiwick. I look out into the glare of the electric lights which extend west as far as I can see, and observe the sidewalks crowded with pedestrians going and returning nobody can tell whither; while scores of cable-cars are gliding noiselessly and constantly, bearing their burdens of humanity to and from the same nameless destination. The sound and sight are not familiar or pleasing, and somehow I want to get away from and forget them; so I will stop writing and retire within the sacred privacy of my inner chamber to read awhile and then woo balmy sleep. Good night.

X.

MENLO PARK AND THE SANTA CLARA VALLEY—*Monterey and the Hotel del Monte—Gov. Stanford's Home and Horses—Some California Landscapes—The Picturesque City—Historic Adobes—An Interesting Drive.*

HOTEL DEL MONTE,
MONTEREY, CAL., June 4th.

I confess to great reluctance in attempting to write this letter. It should be one of exceeding interest, yet the way to make it so does not appear entirely plain before me. I feel as one might be supposed to who has misappropriated or squandered his possessions and finds himself without any reserve in the hour of need. I have used up all my superlatives where occasion appeared to demand them, and to my dismay the real necessity has but just put in an appearance. I was stupid enough to go into ecstasies over the situation at Sierra Madre Villa, where they have flower gardens by the acre and roses which measure five inches in diameter. Alas for my innocence! And when this valley of the Santa Clara comes up for notice, and they show me landscape gardening as a fine art, measuring its extent in square miles, the size of its rose trees by the cord, and its roses so large that they have to be cut before they can be worked into bouquets, there are no figures left — nothing but a few "dittos" or a box or two of turned commas. This hotel from which I write stands in the midst of a park of one hundred and twenty-six acres, every inch of which is under the personal supervision of the most accomplished landscape gardener in the world. It is simply a miracle of beauty. Everything that refined taste can suggest, or that wealth, aided by nature and art, can secure, is here to add to the charms of this delightful spot. The beautiful bay of Monterey washes its northern border ; lofty pines and spreading oaks, and graceful palms, and sweet-scented buckeyes, and the brilliant pepper tree, give grateful shade to walk and lawn; the hotel, with its hundred gables and cornices and verandas, rises in symmetrical proportions amid an ocean of flowers, which cluster and climb and revel over its walls and through its lattices, and up to its very eaves; while the wide-spreading surface of the great park is like a velvet carpet on which are worked in colors of surpassing richness such designs as best please the eye, and are in most perfect harmony with their respective surroundings. But, before I attempt any description of this particular locality, you should know something of the trip hither and its incidents.

The party were to leave San Francisco for Monterey, one hundred and twenty-five miles distant, at four o'clock Monday afternoon. Six gentlemen of the party, including your correspondent, left by the morning train, stopping over for a few hours at Menlo Park, twenty-six miles from San Francisco, and a locality of considerable repute, as you will see. Menlo Park received its name from one of its pioneer settlers, a Doctor Oliver, who came from Ireland, where he owned a tract of land called by the same name. The town has among its inhabitants no less than twenty-two millionaires, including ex-Governor Stanford, J. C. Flood, Mrs. Mark Hopkins, Edgar Mills, the banker, Mrs. F. D. Atherton, Mrs. T. H. Selby, Hon. C. M. Felton, J. A. Donohue, the banker of San Francisco and New York, John T. Doyle, Mrs. Joseph McDonald, and Mrs. J. B. Coleman, both among the O'Brien heirs, Judge H. P. Cohn, Colonel Eyers, the broker of San Francisco, Hon. R. C. Johnson, and others whose names are less familiar. Each of these is the owner of a country seat, and the great number and extent of these palaces and grounds give to Menlo Park an exceptionally attractive appearance and a wide reputation. The finest residence among them all is that of J. C. Flood. As the entrance to his grounds was closed, we could not approach the house nearer than the street, half a mile from the structure itself. As it towered in the distance, above the surrounding trees, it had the appearance of a large public institution, being painted white in resemblance to marble, and having quite an extensive dome and cupola. The grounds are said to be very handsomely laid out and cultivated. We were able to drive through the park and ranch of Governor Stanford, which is probably the largest of any, containing six thousand acres. It is impossible to convey any proper idea of the elegance of the private grounds of these California millionaires. It is like the elegance of Saratoga, except that the climate and soil of this valley render the possibilities here greater than at the East. There is the same wealth of flowers everywhere, and the grand old trees with the clinging moss, and whatever special charm the taste of the owner or his gardener can devise. The Governor has for a year or two past been beautifying a plat of five hundred acres, near his present residence, with a view to erecting a new and more magnificent home. The recent death of his only son has, however, determined him to change his plans. The son was greatly beloved, and is said to have been a most worthy and accomplished young man. Governor Stanford has now determined to erect a free educational institute for young men on the site of his proposed residence, and to maintain it as a memorial of his son. We visited the immense stables of the Governor, where he keeps six hundred and eighty of his horses. They are probably the finest and most costly collection in the country. Among them is the stallion Electioneer, for which he has refused repeated offers of $100,000. We saw also six other stallions of local note, which cost their owner respectively $40,000, $36,000, three $30,000 each, and one $24,000. There were over a hundred fine thoroughbred yearling and two years old colts, neither of which could be bought for a thousand dollars. I know men in Hartford who would give big money to go through these barns and talk horse with Major Rathbun, the accomplished head of the establishment and the trusted lieutenant of Governor Stanford. By the way, this is the identical Major Rathbun who was in the theater box with President Lincoln when the latter was assassinated. The half day spent in sight-seeing at Menlo Park gave me a better idea of the homes of the wealthy in this part of the country than I have ever had. Many of them maintain establishments also in San Francisco, like Stoneman, and Flood, and Hopkins, and Atherton, and others, dividing their time between city and country without regard to season.

At half past four we joined our friends on the "Daisy train" to Monterey. The ride of a hundred miles through the lovely Santa Clara Valley, was one of great attractiveness. Fields of barley and other grains succeeded vineyards almost the entire distance. In the valley proper, which averages about twenty miles wide, the soil is black, and deep, and rich. Wherever covered with crops the verdure is of a very dark green, as is also the foliage of the trees. The mountains on either side rise gradually, and their slopes present a magnificent picture, the shades of green on crest and gorge contrasting harmoniously with the tints imparted by the many-colored wild-flowers growing everywhere. If we had not become so accustomed to these marvelous landscapes, and should see a faithful painting of either of a thousand views which have to-day passed under our notice, we should doubtless declare the coloring extravagant. A California landscape, at this season certainly, is warm and bright, and many-hued, and intoxicatingly beautiful. Without the faintest suspicion of fatigue we rounded the shore of the Bay of Monterey at half past seven, and before dark were in our respective rooms at the Hotel del Monte, the cleanest, sweetest, most homelike, and thus the most heavenly place of refuge that it has been our good or ill fortune to encounter during the progress of this trip. It is an immense establishment, but evidently under good management. Unlike the seaside resorts of the East, this is open the year round, its attractions within and without being the same in January as in July. The hotel is within sound of the ocean surf, and but a few steps from the beach of Monterey Bay. It has a fine bathing pavilion, where are four immense tanks, in each of which the water is of different temperature, and the bather can take his choice. In the pavilion are more than two hundred dressing-rooms, one-half of which are for ladies, each being also provided with fresh-water shower baths. The fine sandy beach outside is utilized by swimmers who prefer the open sea and long distances. The park surrounding the Del Monte has, probably, no equal in this country, if in any country, for the extent and variety of its natural and artificial adornments, in the way of banks, and trees, and flowers, and singing birds, and rare plants, its aviary, and fountains, and club house, its shady nooks, its "maze," its lawns for croquet and tennis, its bicycle runs,— its everything that can minister to the comfort or the enjoyment of sojourners within its delightful area. The house itself is very attractive. It is of ornamental Gothic architecture, can easily accommodate five hundred guests, and is handsomely furnished. It has the special merits of thorough cleanliness, an excellent table, and the best of beds. The very atmosphere of the house and all its surroundings invites to luxurious repose. Unlike San Francisco, the climate is delicious, the air pure and dry, and not subject to the daily winds which prevail higher up the coast.

Monterey, within which municipality this property is situate, lies a mile away, at the southern horn of the crescent which is outlined by the coast of the bay of the same name; Santa Cruz lying at the northern extremity. The old town is most picturesquely placed, and the selection of the site certainly reflects much credit upon the good taste of the Jesuit Father who established here in 1770 the second of the Franciscan Missions founded in this State. There is not much beyond its lovely site to commend Monterey to the notice of the modern tourist, except its history,—and that does not extend far enough back to make it interesting to one so recently from Santa Fé, a city of about three times its age, and infinitely ahead of it in those architectural absurdities which make old American towns interesting. The few remaining adobe houses in Monterey should have a history. They are the Barracks, the Fort, the Custom House, the Catholic Church, the Convent, and half a dozen others. We stood half an hour or more taking on and airing our familiarity with ancient American history, in front of what had been pointed out to us as the Barracks, but which turned out to be only an old Mexican boarding-house. It is quite essential, in looking up antiquities in Monterey, that your information be gathered from a reliable source. The old Custom House is the most conspicuous of all these historic edifices. It is well preserved, and still has, pointing skyward from its northern gable, the original flag-staff from which floated the first American flag that was hoisted in California after its acquisition by the United States Government.

There are delightful drives from the Hotel del Monte in various directions, but the most interesting is that which takes the tourist through Monterey and into Pacific Grove, skirting the ocean from Shell Beach to Pebble Beach, over the eighteen or twenty miles of road lying within the Hotel Company's private grounds. Along this coast are found the beautiful abalone and other sea shells, in great variety of form and color. Many of us have spent hours in searching for the most beautiful specimens, and in looking for the rare "lucky stone" of Pebble Beach. There are several barrels of these shells now in possession of our party, most of which will probably have to be left when the time of our final departure comes. There are seal rocks here, also, though not harboring as large a colony of seals as those at the Cliff House opposite San Francisco. The moss-hung oaks and cedars, which are seen at several points on the road, constitute objects of much interest; so do the banks of wild-flowers which are sure to present themselves wherever the rich loam shows a little sand or clay.

We expect to dwell here, delightedly, until Saturday, June seventh. Then we shall return to San Francisco, and make our ultimate exit from that point. If, as anticipated, I conclude to take in Santa Cruz and San Jose during the present week, it may give occasion for another letter before we leave California.

XI.

A Long-to-be-remembered week — *Farewell to Del Monte and Monterey—A Day at Santa Cruz—Some Big, Big Trees—An Old Tannery—San Jose—Squinting Eastward.*

Palace Hotel,
San Francisco, Cal., June 8th.

The phenomenon of a rainy Sunday in a California summer kindly interferes with an engagement which I made last evening to attend church to-day with a friend. I deem the interference kindly because the morning finds me thoroughly tired by the unusual activities of the last two days; and, much as I should enjoy an hour with Doctor Stone, the rest and retirement of my own room will be better for me physically, though morally and intellectually I chance to be the loser.

We are here for a farewell look at San Francisco and the Pacific Coast, for within a day or two the Raymond Party will face and forward march toward home. A long-to-be-remembered week have we spent at the Hotel del Monte, and amid the attractions of which it is the hub and center. I have spoken well of del Monte. The place fully deserves such mention. I rather like, too, the quiet old town of Monterey, and find that there is much about it after all to fascinate a person who has plenty of time to look it over and mouse among its antiquities. The town was evidently once a place of considerable importance. Its numerous streets are now scarcely more than relics of former greatness, for many of them are grass-grown and bordered by ruins of what were once the habitations and places of business of generations long since gone the way of all flesh. Mounds of earth in several localities only remain of what may have been pretentious adobes a century ago; and the old

Main Street, now scarcely better than a cow-path, has but an occasional building and a few mud-crowned and moss-grown corrals, to mark the thoroughfare which was doubtless the center of population and traffic in the palmy days of old Spanish rule. What little remained of business activity or of population, has gravitated nearer the beach, and there is small hope that the deserted district higher up the pleasant acclivity will ever be reclaimed.

Monterey has its Chinese Quarter, which, by the way, should never be visited by the tourist except on a full stomach. The sole industry of the Quarter consists in drying squid, or "devil fish," for exportation to China. The atmosphere is abominable. It furnishes a strong argument that "the Chinese should go." No other community makes merchandise of so foul and stinking a product as dried squid.

I found a genius at Monterey, in the person of Mr. T. G. Lambert, a notary public, justice of the peace, and lumber merchant. He lives in the old Custom House, one of the historic adobes of the city. His wife runs a shell store, and does a thriving trade with the del Monte's guests. You see he has an eye for the main chance; that is because he is a Massachusetts Yankee. He has been on this coast thirty-eight years. He is a Blaine man all through. He paid fifty-eight dollars into the State treasury yesterday for knocking down an Irishman who said Blaine was a d—d rascal. He paid the money cheerfully; and is now looking for further opportunities of the same sort. I like his earnestness, but cannot commend his method of defending political friends.

I am under obligation to Mr. Harding, the obliging manager of the party, for a very agreeable drive in his private carriage during the afternoon of Friday. Mr. Harding has spent a large part of the past year at the Hotel del Monte, and is familiar with all points of interest in the vicinity. We visited the Lighthouse, all the Beaches on the ocean side, Cypress Point, Cape Horn, the Reservoir, Pacific Grove Retreat and Camp Ground, Carmel Mission Church, drove through all the streets of old Monterey and Chinatown, and to the old and new Cemeteries of the city. Of course we observed many objects of interest which had been unheeded in our previous ride with a hireling driver. The managers of these Raymond Parties seem to be constantly on the alert for opportunities, not on the itineraries, to increase the comforts and enjoyments of their tourists. How well they succeed is illustrated in the frequent graceful favors which I have had occasion to acknowledge from Mr. Harding and his assistants.

Saturday morning eight of us took a six o'clock breakfast and left by early train for a day at Santa Cruz, arriving at the beach station soon after nine o'clock. Santa Cruz has long been the most popular and fashionable seaside resort on the Pacific Coast.

Although the town has a population of but five or six thousand, the influx of visitors during some months of the year often swells the number of actual inhabitants to ten thousand. It is situated, nominally, on Monterey Bay, although so well on to the cape at its entrance as to be really as much an ocean as a bay town. In its location, as well as its composition, it is thoroughly picturesque; and it is a common remark of tourists that it is among the pleasantest places in California. Grace Greenwood happily described it in a few words when she wrote, some years ago: "Santa Cruz is a beautiful, smiling town, seated on the knees of pleasant terraces with her feet in the sea." Many of the private residences in the heart of the city, and the clusters of cottages in the suburbs, are embowered in roses, which grow to wonderful size and in great profusion. We spent but an hour or two in the city, only observing enough of its scenery to occasion regret that days instead of hours had not been assigned for the visit.

The main object of this incidental trip to Santa Cruz was to see Big Tree Grove, which lies eight miles up the San Lorenzo River, and is reached by a narrow gauge railroad or by carriage. We employed the latter medium, partly because of a preference for the carriage drive through the picturesque San Lorenzo Defile, but chiefly because the narrow-gauge train had already departed when we were ready to start. The drive to the Grove occupied little more than an hour, and proved to be even more agreeable than had been anticipated, the road being good, the weather delightful, and the scenery positively enchanting. At the Grove we found a great number of visitors from San Francisco, and several parties encamped in tents on the banks of the adjacent stream. The big trees consist of perhaps a score of immense specimens, with hundreds of smaller ones, all of the California red-wood, and exceedingly shapely in form. The largest is "The

Giant," which measures sixty-six feet in circumference, and is three hundred and forty feet high as it stands. Some weeks ago a gale of wind broke twenty-four feet from the top—its previous height having been three hundred and seventy-four feet. It is a good, honest tree, and the measurement here given is of *bona fide* trunk, not of root extensions. Its height to the first branch is about one hundred and twenty feet, or more than the entire height of most of the tallest trees of New England. Another large tree is the "General Fremont." This is sixty-three feet in circumference and three hundred and ten feet high. The lower fifteen feet of the trunk is hollow, and its interior measures upon the ground twenty-four feet eight inches in its largest, and eighteen feet in its smallest diameter. Forty-six men have stood upright within it at one time, and our little party of twelve found abundant room for circulating about within its walls without jostling each other in the least. When this Grove was first discovered, in 1840, a Mexican family were living in this hollow tree, and it is known that several children were born there. In '46, when General Fremont was at Santa Cruz, he made his headquarters in the tree for a short time, which fact furnished a reason for giving it his name. The interior is approached through an aperture cut in the trunk, about three by six feet in size, and is lighted by three holes or windows, each about two feet square. The thickness of the shell, including wood and bark, as I measured it with my walking-stick, is about two and a half feet. The interior surface of the trunk, as high as a man can reach, is covered with the cards of visitors. Of course, each of our party contributed his individual pasteboard to the collection. "Jumbo" is another large specimen, so called from a gnarled spot on one face of the trunk which resembles an elephant's head. "The Three

Sisters" stand side by side, two or three feet apart, a cavity through the middle tree being used as an ice cream saloon in which several persons may easily sit around a table therein, where ice cream and cake are served. Other almost equally large trees have local names, and some of them a curious local history. An old giant, lying prone upon the ground, once served as a tan vat, a rude tannery being located here when the Grove was discovered by white men. The huge trunk lies there, one hundred feet in length, and of an almost uniform size from one end to the other. In this trunk are cut four vats, each twenty feet long and five feet deep and about seven feet wide. The sides of the vats are considerably decayed and broken, but their shape and dimensions are easily marked. This old tree, lying by its stump, in the same position that it fell and was used half a century ago, forms an interesting relic of an age which ante-dates civilization on this part of the Pacific Coast. The tract of real estate on which the Big Tree Grove is located, is owned by the railroad company, and the Grove is leased to a Mr. Aldrich, who keeps the grounds in condition, provides entertainment for visitors, and has photographic views of the trees for sale. He is very polite in his attentions, and thoroughly reasonable in his charges. The attraction which this locality possesses for tourists and others is indicated by the great number of visitors who come here, sometimes a thousand in a single day. I have made no incidental excursion during the progress of this trip, which has been more gratifying in its results, or will be recalled with greater pleasure, than this day at the Big Tree Grove of Santa Cruz.

I have felt a little disappointment in not being able to mature plans for putting in a day at San Jose. Having passed through the city twice, and had glowing descriptions of its beauty from those familiar with it, I am quite sure that I have lost something in failing to visit the place. It is in the very richest part of the Santa Clara Valley, is celebrated for its floral attractions, its fruit orchards, and its fine streets. Cherries and other small fruit, as well as flowers and trees, are at their best just now, and the situation must be enchanting to the palate as well as to the eye. But we are too far from San Jose now to think of a visit this time; some other time, perhaps.

As before intimated, we feel as if the Raymond Excursion to the Pacific were drawing to a close. We are here again in San Francisco to prepare for the return East; and when we finally get started in that direction there will be few and short stops this side of our ultimate destination. I shall probably address you a letter from Salt Lake City, but that will be the last. This has been a trip of sight-seeing, and not for letter-writing; and I often entertain regrets that any attempt has been made by me to record observations or experiences by the way. With time to do it well, the story could have been made interesting and profitable; as it is, it may, perhaps, prove a momentary gratification to some of us who have participated, but nothing more.

XII.

GOOD-BYE TO SAN FRANCISCO—*Again in the Pullmans—Over the Sierra Nevadas—Rounding Cape Horn—Charming Mountain Scenery—Hydraulic Mining—Christening a Papoose—Salt Lake City—In the Mormon Tabernacle—Eighty-One Babies.*

SALT LAKE CITY, UTAH, June 15th.

The last two or three days in San Francisco were busy ones for the Raymond Party. There were farewell visits to be made among friends, final tramps and drives about the city and its environs, a long list of engagements to fill, and many souvenirs to be purchased. They were trying days for many a plethoric pocket book; and I do not doubt that the trinket dealers of Kearney and Montgomery and

Market Streets, and the Chinese Quarter, were made fully a thousand dollars happier during the shopping tours of the ladies and gentlemen on Monday and Tuesday, and Wednesday morning. I employed the time chiefly in trips to the Presidio and the Golden Gate, taking one more look through Woodward's Gardens, a climb to the top of the observatory on Telegraph Hill, and a run over to Oakland—one of the prettiest cities, by the way, on this or any other continent. On the morning of our departure I chanced to read in the morning paper something about Judge Toohy's rulings, and it occurred to me that Judge Toohy is a brother of the celebrated Hartford auctioneer of the same name. So I posted off in the rain to the old City Hall, near the corner of Kearney and Washington Streets, and found the Judge just leaving the Superior Court Chambers. The mention of William Toohy as my friend and acquaintance, proved a passport to the hospitality of the big-hearted judge, and his welcome was so sincere and cordial as to make it very hard for me to extend greetings and adieus, as I was obliged to, in almost the same breath. I shall never forget the warmth of his handshaking as he bowed me out of his sanctum and wished me "a safe and delightful journey back to old Hartford!" We shall all take with us many pleasant recollections of our stay in San Francisco, which, despite its chilly winds and the phenomenal rain storm with which we left it deluged, is a city that bears acquaintance wonderfully well.

We took our last lunch at the Palace Hotel at noon of Wednesday, and shortly afterward were summoned for rendezvous in the court-yard corridors, from whence the coaches of the United Carriage Company conveyed the party to the Oakland ferry. Four miles across the bay we found in waiting for us two of the elegant buffet boudoir cars of the Pullman Company, which our thoughtful manager had provided in order that we might enjoy well-cooked and well-served meals in transit between San Francisco and Salt Lake City, in lieu of the uncertain accommodations of border hotels and restaurants. One who has not had the experience can hardly appreciate the satisfaction which attended our reunion in the Pullmans which we had learned to regard as home on the outward trip. Doubtless the fact that we were now heading homeward, with nearer anticipations of the welcome awaiting us from loved ones, had something to do with the general good feeling manifest in smiling faces and kindly greetings and extra-obliging manners. I am sure the weather was in no sense responsible, for the rain poured with a persistence which threatened to imperil railroad travel as it was jeopardizing the hay crop exposed to view in our progress up the coast of San Pablo Bay. In good time we made the straits of Carquinez, where the mammoth ferry boat Solano, the largest craft of its kind in the world, takes the entire train across to Benicia. Through vineyards and orchards and waving grain fields we went leisurely on to Sacramento, and at Colfax halted, the cars remaining stationary on the track through the night in order that we might make the transit of the next one hundred miles by daylight, through the region of some of the most romantic scenery on the continent. For over fourteen hundred miles of our journey from Colfax eastward, through California, Nevada, Utah, Wyoming and a portion of Nebraska, our path is at an elevation of from two thousand five hundred to over eight thousand feet above the sea level. Along here, as we cross the Sierra Nevadas, the altitude is from five to seven thousand feet. For much of the time we are actually among snow banks, and for several days in succession we appear to be surrounded and hemmed in by mountains whose rugged sides and summits lie deep buried under the accumulated snows of generations and perhaps centuries. As the train winds around the hill sides, among intricate passes, through dark cañons, over trestles and into tunnels, it seems as if we must be hopelessly lost, and it becomes a standing wonder how a railroad could ever be located here. About five miles east of Colfax the train passes around the point familiarly known as "Cape Horn." It is a projection of the rocky mountain side on which the road had to be constructed upon a kind of shelf; and as the train halts for a moment on the very brink, one may look down almost vertically two thousand two hundred feet, to the bed of the American River below, where the stream appears in the deep distance to be scarcely more than a little brook.

We get magnificent views for many miles of our route through this American Cañon. The gorges are of vast depth and extent; the mountains covered with tall trees up to the timber line, and with eternal snow above it; the waterfalls and mountain streams come tumbling down in surprising volume; with now and then little valleys where wild flowers spring, as if nature had dropped her fancy morning robe among the hills, or thrown out some of her best parlor carpets for an airing. The long snow sheds, covering an extent of forty miles, obstruct the views on both sides in a most exasperating manner, but whenever the train stops for a moment—as for some cause it often does—we do not fail to alight and catch glimpses through the cracks and seams of the heavy plank sides. One of the very prettiest landscapes at this great elevation takes in Donner Lake, which nestles among the peaks just east of the summit. It is about four miles long by one and a half broad, and lies at an altitude of six thousand seven hundred and forty-nine feet above the sea. Its waters are like crystal, and its pebbly beach is as fine as can be imagined. The railroad approaches to within about a hundred yards of its margin. Its location is such as to render a nearer approach almost impossible. I do not suppose there is a human habitation within a great many miles of it. At Dutch Flat, Blue Cañon, and east as well as west of the divide, are extensive traces of hydraulic mining. Thousands of acres are covered with the débris of hills and rock elevations which have been reduced and swept away under huge streams of water conveyed through pipes and conduits. This débris covers broad plains or stands like huge sentinels in spots to mark where once the mountain stood. The aggregate of earth which toiling miners have thus removed in their laborious search for gold, is simply stupendous. Perhaps I do not need to explain to you what hydraulic mining is. The miner selects his claim, which may be a gravel hill, one or two hundred feet high and covering an area of ten or twenty acres. To find the gold contained in this hill by the old method, the whole elevation must be shoveled over and examined. But the hydraulic miner makes a reservoir at a high altitude on a neighboring mountain, and through an iron pipe plays water from the reservoir on to the hill as a fireman would play through his hose upon a burning building. He sends sometimes a four or six-inch stream, under five hundred feet head. Under such influences his gravel hill gets washed away with great rapidity, while the saving of manual labor is several hundred per cent.

We spent Thursday night at Truckee, and took breakfast next morning at Reno, the first station in Nevada east of California. I shall remember Reno, because of its delightful situation on a pretty crowning plateau, surrounded by snowy mountains, which the rising sun gilded until they looked like fire opals in the hazy heights above. I shall remember it, also, because of the fine flavor of the salmon trout which constituted the first course of our breakfast at the station dining-hall. Granite Point, an otherwise insignificant station, ninety miles beyond, was rendered memorable by the appearance of an Indian squaw with her one-week-old papoose, in a wicker cage, on her back. She was begging for the papoose. Her chief desire seemed to be for cookies. We had no cookies, nor other edibles adapted for so young a child, so we gave it simply a name. We christened the papoose Charles T. Almy, in honor of an honorable and esteemed member of our party. The wigwams of the Piute and Shoshone Indians are frequently seen along the line of the railroad, and their occupants put in an appearance at about every station. The Indians are allowed to ride on the freight trains of this road without payment of fares. We were at Humboldt in time for dinner. For over three hundred miles the railroad traverses the Humboldt Valley, by the margin of the Humboldt River, and under the shadow of the Humboldt Range of mountains. This Humboldt River, which is a stream of about the volume of your Farmington River, is five hundred miles in length, empties into a small lake, known as "Humboldt Sink," and thus disappears, as the lake has no outlet. Friday afternoon we made two hundred miles before darkness shut out the series of magnificent views among the mountains and palisades, which rendered the day and ride memorable. Friday evening found us eating strawberries and cream, mountain trout and baked potatoes, with orange fritters and coffee, at the little station restaurant at Elko. Friday night, while we slept, our trusty engineer made the run of the Great American Desert in northeastern Nevada and northwestern Utah. At daybreak we came in sight of Great Salt Lake, and skirted its coast for thirty miles. Ogden was reached in time for an early breakfast, and half an hour given us in which to observe and admire the natural attractions of this second city of importance in the territory. It lies at the head of the beautiful valley which extends south beyond Salt Lake City, is protected by high mountains on three sides, penetrated by numerous cañons which constitute avenues of approach for railroads from at least four points of the compass. It is a busy place, and delightful to behold in its setting of green and white mountain scenery, with the spreading valley at its feet and the blue lake in the distance. At Ogden we diverge from the direct route, for the purpose of visiting Salt Lake City, the capital of Mormondom, thirty-seven miles directly south. The route lies through a fertile valley, which is dotted here and there with little white houses, to the number of several hundred. In the distance we see the main road up the valley filled with single and double wagons, loaded with men, women and children, all going toward Ogden. Inquiry reveals the secret of the exodus; there was to be a circus.

A clock, somewhere, is striking the hour

of nine as our train makes the first halt, and we find ourselves in the midst of Zion, as the Latter Day Saints denominate their city. The Mormon metropolis is a city of somewhat more than twenty thousand inhabitants, three-quarters of whom are Mormons. The great Temple is in the center of the city, and the streets, which run at right angles, are all named and numbered from it. The streets are wide and lined with shade trees, brooks of living water from the mountains running in trenches upon either side of every avenue, and serving to irrigate as well the yards and gardens. On the north and east rise the rugged spurs of the Wahsatch Mountains, on the south and west the broad and fertile valley extends twenty or thirty miles, and away to the northwest lies the Great Salt Lake, or inland sea, ninety-five miles long, thirty miles broad, and at an elevation of four thousand two hundred and sixty feet above the level of the ocean. We lose no time in making up little exploring parties to the various points which demand attention. Through the courtesy of Hon. Guido Marx, your correspondent made the tour of the city in distinguished company and under the pilotage of a well-informed and attentive coachman. We drove through all the streets, our particular attention being called to the original residence and to the grave of Brigham Young, the "Bee Hive" and the "Lion," the Amelia Palace, the homes of present church dignitaries, the three houses of Brigham Young, Jr., in which his three wives respectively reside, Camp Douglas, etc. In an enclosure, surrounded by a wall ten feet high, are the Tabernacle, the Assembly House, the Endowment House, and the new Temple, which latter is in an unfinished condition, having been thirty-one years in reaching its present dimensions, and is expected to be completed during the present century. It is to cost ten millions, about half of which has already been expended. Its foundations are sixteen feet thick, its walls, which are of granite, being nine feet and nine inches thick above the foundation. When completed it will be a very substantial and imposing structure. The Tabernacle is a remarkable building. In it the Sunday services are held. It will seat ten thousand persons. It contains an organ which cost one hundred thousand dollars. Its acoustic properties are so perfect that, notwithstanding its immense size, a pin dropped upon the floor at one end of the audience room is distinctly heard by a person standing at the opposite extremity. I attended services in the great Tabernacle this afternoon, and heard Joseph F. Smith blaspheme. Joseph F. is a son of Hiram Smith, and a nephew of the original Joe Smith, prophet and revelator. He occupies in the church the position of second counselor, whatever that may mean. There was, this afternoon, an audience of fully six thousand persons, three-quarters of whom were women. The ordinance of the Lord's Supper is celebrated every Sunday. It took twelve deacons one hour and twenty minutes to-day, to serve the bread and water (not wine). There were eighty-one babies in the congregation, and you may well imagine they accomplished considerable howling, which, however, did not seem to disturb the other exercises in the least. The Mormon women, as they appeared in the Tabernacle, are certainly the worst looking crowd I ever met. It is a mystery to me how a man can endure a plurality of them in the capacity of wife, or any other capacity. There were fifteen or twenty celebrants who took a hand in the ceremonies, but three or four of them did all the talking. Joseph Smith was, evidently, the most cultured of the speakers. He seemed to observe that there were many strangers among his auditors (special seats are reserved for strangers) and to have made up his mind to "give 'em fits." He traduced and maligned all other religious sects and denominations, and extolled the Mormon creed as the conservator of all that is good in faith or practice. He blasphemingly classed Jo. Smith and B. Young with Moses and our Saviour, giving the former priority in the order of classification. It was a shocking exhibition of demagoguery and fanaticism. The music was fine. The great organ, accompanied by a trained choir of nearly two hundred voices, under a leader who knew his business, filled the immense auditorium with music that in its grandeur and sublimity seemed worthy of a more exalted and sacred purpose. Strangely enough, the words and melodies were the same that I have heard in orthodox churches a hundred times.

> "My God is reconciled,
>   His pard'ning voice I hear,
> He owns me for his child,
>   I can no longer fear;
> With confidence I now draw nigh,
> And Father, Abba Father, cry,"

Was rendered with a skill and pathos which

set many a disconsolate looking woman in the audience to sobbing audibly and convulsively. It was a cruel mockery of undefiled religion which made the head faint and the whole heart sick. I have conversed personally with several of these Mormons, and feel thoroughly disgusted with the whole business. If there were space for it in this letter, I could relate incidents which have come to my knowledge or under my observation already, which would lead you to sympathize with me in my unqualified disgust.

We were entertained at the Continental Hotel during the sojourn here. It is a miserable hostelry, untidy in its furnishings, and worse in its cuisine. Yet it is beyond question the best hotel in the city. The commercial houses here are generally quite commonplace in the variety of their merchandise, and by no means pretentious in outside appearances. I have heard much said of the attractiveness of Salt Lake City, but careful observation has failed to detect a single reason, beyond the beauty of situation, for the compliments of this sort which others have bestowed. In no respect, as I observe it, does the city compare favorably with a great many others this side of the Mississippi Valley; and it is so far behind Denver, for instance, as to dwindle in comparison. But we are exceedingly glad of having had an opportunity to see the city, which, by reason of its religion, has become fully as famous as any other city in the old or new world. We shall leave it to-morrow, and unless the rain which threatens to-night comes to interfere with the process, we shall "shake the dust from our feet" in departing, as a testimony against this ungodly and adulterous generation.

XIII.

The Backward Journey—*Social Calls in Mormondom—Mining Interests of Utah—Webber and Echo Cañons—Wonderful Rock Formations—Again the Rockies—Disintegration of the Raymond Party—A Few Things Personal—Home Again.*

Niagara Falls, June 20th.

I bade you good evening last Sunday at Salt Lake City, since which date we have traveled over an additional two thousand five hundred miles of mountain and prairie, and find ourselves within an easy twenty-four hours run of Hartford. Somehow, there doesn't seem to be the same incentive to write details of the homeward as there was of the outward journey; and, although there is quite as much of the novel and wonderful to be seen on the line of the Central and Union as on the Southern Pacific Railroad, I think I shall be able to condense the whole within the limits of this letter.

We left Salt Lake City at three o'clock, Monday afternoon. The morning was devoted to personal investigations of this chief citadel of Mormonism, in such various ways as the inclinations of the investigators seemed to dictate. My own inclination led me, in company with Mr. Fullam, to make a formal call on President Taylor and his wives at their home in the famed Amelia Palace; and further to a personal interview with Joseph F. Smith, the chief apostle, who is alleged to be able to cure diseases and confer the gift of tongues, by the laying on of hands. We attempted a call upon Brigham Young, junior, but absence of that dignitary from the city, and a disinclination of his private secretary to allow strange gentlemen at either of the three houses where his three wives reside, and where he lodges alternately when "at home," interfered with the complete execution of our purpose. At the Amelia Palace we found only the one wife with which the President now lives, and in the absence of the public functionary himself our interview with her was exceedingly brief and thoroughly conventional. We met a most cordial welcome from Counsellor Smith, who is a gentleman of scholarly attainments and of most positive religious sentiments. After making a tour of the tithing houses, and some other of the institutions of the Saints, I dropped in upon Mr. Prescott of *The Daily Tribune* and looked through the mechanical department of his establishment. My last hour in the city was most agreeably spent at the Salt Lake Mining Institute, where I met the polite personal attention of Professor Clayton, who very kindly made up for me a collection of specimens of the ores and minerals of Utah, from the contents of his extensive and admirable museum and laboratory. I shall have something to say hereafter concerning the possibilities of Utah as a mining territory for the precious metals.

Retracing our way to Ogden, the point of intersection with the Union Pacific railroad, we shortly found ourselves headed east and fairly on the home stretch, without expectation of further tarryings or delays on the trip. Supper was eaten at the Ogden Station Hotel, and the train lost as little time as possible in getting off; for the majestic scenery of Webber and Echo Cañons lay all along the route within the next fifty miles, and our anxiety was great to take in the grand exhibition before night should drop its curtain of darkness between us and the panorama. Without even the formality of announcement, the show began in the magnificent rock and mountain scenery all about us, as the train made its first plunge across Webber River, and followed the stream in its tortuous windings into the cañon to which the river gives its name.

The rocky walls which confine the waters became higher and more precipitous, and the general view wilder, until at Devil's Gate the climax is reached, where the river makes a sudden sweep to the north and then to the southeast again, through a mighty chasm which seems to have been opened expressly for the purpose in the immense wall of rock which must have once stood there to dispute the further progress of this rushing torrent. For a dozen miles there is the same succession of rock and ravine and towering height and nestling valley, until shortly the whole thing changes, and behold! a great plain with outcroppings of tremendous cliffs and boulders in weird and fascinating forms of castles and fortresses, and ruined cities, and miles of wall standing where nature built it as if with line and plummet, thirty, forty, fifty feet high, in solid adamant. Near the railroad track we pass the famous Devil's Slide, photographs of which are on exhibition in pretty much every part of the world.

This "slide" is on the face of a high and steep mountain which is covered with verdure. Out of this verdure crop two great parallel walls of rock, about ten feet apart, starting apparently about one-third of a mile up the mountain and continuing at a height of perhaps sixty to seventy feet down to its base. The space between the two walls is not grass-grown, but of a rock-chippy character which would be likely to prove unpleasant even to the Devil should he attempt in *propria personæ* to accomplish the descent without his buckskin pants on. As we approach Echo Cañon the distant elevations appear to be crowned with immense fortresses, perfect in form of rampart and bastion and battlement. The illusion is so complete that beholders often insist that these great natural wonders must be works of art, though a near view is said to completely dispel the illusion. The locality is called Castle Park. A few miles east of it, and almost surrounded by one of the great natural walls before alluded to, is a collection of huge boulders, each of thousands of tons weight, amid which are pretty little fir trees growing. This would be appropriately called Boulder Park, though it is designated by no name. The magnificent and charming localities in this section seem to be too numerous to afford each a name.

A diversion from landscape viewing was here occasioned, for a moment, by the appearance of a bear and two cubs leisurely ascending a foothill of one of the Wahsatch Mountain spurs within easy sight from the car windows. Elk, deer, antelope, buffalo, coyote, and prairie dogs without number, had already rewarded our diligent watch in localities where these respective varieties of wild beasts were supposed to abound, but never before a wild bear. We took breakfast at Rawlins, seven thousand feet above the sea. Eagles' nests in the cliffs are a frequent sight, on many of which the parent bird is easily discerned. The Rockies, still snow-covered, present again their familiar peaks. We have been in sight of snow every day for more than five weeks, or ever since the day of our arrival at Manitou. At Carbon station are extensive coal fields. Coal mining is the sole industry of the people of this particular region. Dinner at Laramie, in sight of the Black Hills, from which first named place a stage route runs direct to Deadwood. Again a series of strange rock formations, unlike any of those already seen, among them the Red Buttes, a most remarkable formation. It is as if some children of giants had made a thousand red mud palaces, and towers, and monuments, and mushrooms, and tigers and lions, and elephants, and other representatives of things living and inanimate, each a hundred or more feet high and all of the same bright red mud, and had set them up on a great plain, where after centuries they had successively hardened and begun to crumble. We see them now at the crumbling stage. They are a strange creation, and to me the most unexpected, so to speak, of anything I have seen. At Sherman we reach the summit of our climb over the Rocky Mountains. Here we find the pyramidal monument erected in honor of Oakes Ames, the projector of the Central Pacific Railroad. Six or seven miles east of Sherman stands the most remarkable of all the wonderful natural fortresses thus far observed. It crowns the summit of a great elevation on the north of the railroad, and covers apparently a square mile of dead level. Years hence it will be classed among the great natural curiosities of the world. In proximity to it is a great boulder park similar to one already mentioned. I regard the trouble and inconvenience and expense of this trip as fully compensated by the unique and startling exhibitions, done in granite and sandstone, which have excited our surprise and admiration at every point between Ogden and the eastern slope of the Rockies.

We reached Cheyenne in time for supper, having approached it for thirty miles over a delightful bit of prairie which extended to the horizon, without stones, or trees, or bushes, or hillocks,—simply a great green grassy plain. Darkness deprives us of anticipated observations between Cheyenne and the Nebraska line, but the train drives on by night as well as by day, and we wake Wednesday morning to find ourselves in a region of farm-houses and barns, and fenced pastures, and fields of corn and wheat, and fruit and shade trees, and such general evidences of civilization as we have not seen since leaving the valley of the Great Salt Lake. This is Central Nebraska. We reach Grand Island in time for breakfast. This is the first uncomfortably warm weather we have encountered. We have found more and warmer since. Watches are set ahead another hour before reaching Grand Island, to correspond with local time. Dinner at Omaha; mercury at ninety in the shade.

Crossed the mile-and-a-quarter bridge over the Missouri between Omaha and Council Bluffs; and lest I appear to thus unduly dignify the "Big Muddy," which at this point is not as wide as the Connecticut at Hartford, let me add that more than half of this bridge is over a marsh or a mud bank. From Council Bluffs, eastward three hundred and sixteen miles, to Davenport, we run across the beautiful farming lands of Iowa. At every station we observe acres of corn cribs filled with corn on the ear. Every rod of land seems to be under cultivation, which is in striking contrast with Nevada, Wyoming, or even Nebraska, where are untold millions of acres without an owner or occupant to turn up one shovel-full of its yet undiscovered subsoil. I understand now how easy it must be for a man who enjoys farming or stock-raising, to go into ecstasies when he gets into such a region as Iowa, where he is confronted by a wealth of soil never dreamed of in New England, with foliage and grain fields and gardens of superlative strength and stateliness of growth, almost without other effort than simply casting the seed upon the surface of mother earth. But, much as I enjoy the products of agriculture, of the garden, the orchard, the vineyard, or even the flower beds and the orange groves, I can find no delight in any of the processes involved. Excuse the confession; it is gratuitous, and very likely implies a low condition of manliness. I had a taste of farming in very early life which proved as satisfying as a full meal.

We reached Davenport at eight o'clock Thursday morning, and from that point our return has been over precisely the same route as that taken by the party on its outward trip. At three P. M. the same day we were at Chicago, where we were given a rest of five hours with supper at the Sherman House. Resuming our places in the sleeper shortly after eight o'clock, we proceeded by the Grand Trunk, expecting to reach Port

Huron before daylight. A crippled freight train on our path twenty miles out of Chicago, delayed us, however, several hours, and we barely reached Lansing, Mich., at half past seven Friday morning, stopping at Durand for breakfast an hour later. We crossed the great St. Clair River, or straits, at Port Huron, by ferry, occupying an hour in the transit. Thence to Niagara Falls direct, reaching and crossing Suspension Bridge at fifteen minutes past eight in the evening, too near dark to get more than a glimpse of the outline of the great cataract. We feel a little disappointed at the delays which set us down here six hours behind time, for we had hoped to be able go ashore and get a nearer and more satisfactory view of Niagara than can be obtained from Suspension Bridge or any other point on the railroad. But I am sure the management and the train hands have done every thing in their power, though unsuccessfully, to help us out of the trouble forced upon our party by the derailed freight. From this point we shall proceed by the West Shore & Buffalo Railway to Rotterdam Junction, thence by the Hoosac Tunnel and Fitchburg Roads to Greenfield, the Connecticut River Road to Springfield, and our own Consolidated Road to Hartford. If we have good luck I shall be with you at seven forty Saturday evening.

The party, which left Boston more than sixty strong, is pretty well broken up even at this point. Of the original number, three dropped out at Santa Fé, one at Colorado Springs, three at Monterey, eight at San Francisco, two at Truckee, two at Omaha, one at West Liberty in Iowa, one at Davenport, eighteen at Chicago, one left us here at Niagara, four will leave at Greenfield, two at Gardner, five at Ayer Junction, only thirteen remaining to go through to Boston.

And now, as this two months of pleasuring among eighteen states and territories is about to terminate, let me say a few things personal of the party in whose more or less intimate companionship the long journey has been accomplished, and with most of whom I have already exchanged the final hand-shakings and spoken the good-by words.

I do not believe that a party of kinder-hearted or more considerate gentlemen and ladies ever crossed the continent in company. The situation has been uniformly pleasant, and often under adverse circumstances when the good nature of the party and of the management was severely tested. I wish to make particular mention of my early and well esteemed Connecticut friends, Dr. Pinney and Mr. Merriman, with their estimable ladies; Mr. Whidden of Boston, whose pleasant face, and that of his son, I shall hope to see often in the future; Mr. Fish of Brooklyn, N. Y., my most frequent companion in tramps and seances without number; Hon. Mr. Marx and family of

Toledo; Mr. Hamilton and family of Philadelphia; Mr. Valpey and wife of Lynn; Mr. and Mrs. Howe, Mrs. Brown, the Worcester delegation of gentlemen and ladies, to all of whom I am indebted for constant personal courtesies. I shall never cease to recall pleasant memories of days and nights in the same section with my robust partner, Mr. C. T. Almy, where the former were enlivened by his inimitable stories, and the latter by his equally inimitable snoring. And I must not neglect a modest allusion to the kind-hearted and irrepressible Mrs. Nichols, whose repeated request to "put my name in your letter," is at length affirmatively heeded. I take the liberty of calling these names because they happen to represent a few with whom I became most familiar; if I felt equal freedom with others it would be an easy and pleasant task to connect the name of each of our sixty odd tourists with some interesting situation or incident of the trip, which we who participated should recognize at a glance. Such action would, however, be unpardonable in this correspondence, and I will not attempt it. I am ready to give a testimonial in favor of every railroad over which we have traveled, although you will grant that I have not lumbered up your columns with puffs of this or any other description. Permit me in closing to express the opinion of our entire company in favor of the excellent management which has not only taken us over eight thousand five hundred miles of territory, some of it in places of great peril, and now returned us to our homes without an accident of the slightest magnitude, but that has succeeded in transforming a long and tiresome ride into a delightful excursion and a constant picnic.

I re-open this letter, as the train is approaching Hartford, to remark that the hills and valleys and streams and people of Connecticut never looked so good to me as now.

Home again! Back from the land of gold and silver and "bits," to the land also of greenbacks and good honest dimes, and nickels and pennies! Back to the land of men and women, as well as of mountains and mines and prairies! Back to my home, and all it contains and signifies! I would not exchange one county of old Connecticut for whole states in the far west, unless I could sell out at my own price on acquiring the new possession. I wish, more than ever, to visit every part of our immense and wonderful country, but New England shall ever contain the home to which I will return again!

J. A. S.

REUNION.

While in transit from Ogden to Chicago, a formal meeting of the excursionists was held, to provide for one or more reunions after the return of the party to their respective homes. A permanent organization of the "Raymond Pacific Excursion Party of April 24, 1884," was effected by the appointment of Thos. J. Whidden as President, Mrs. J. E. Bacon, Vice-President, E. A. Merriman, Secretary, and Chas. T. Almy, Treasurer. It was voted to hold a reunion at the call of the Secretary, and the four officers above named were authorized to name the place and date.

www.ingramcontent.com/pod-product-compliance
Lightning Source LLC
Chambersburg PA
CBHW021732220426
43662CB00008B/809